A MATTER OF STYLE

Intimate Portraits of 10 Women Who Changed Fashion

WHITE STAR PUBLISHERS

Foreword

by Valeria Manferto De Fabianis

A matter of style. The secret is encapsulated in these words. Many women dedicate their heart and soul to their image, through careful choice of makeup, cut and color of hair, to finding unique and exclusive dresses, and to collecting loads of accessories. In doing so, many manage to achieve a certain level of elegance. But few – very few – are able to create their own style, a style that transcends fashions and stereotypes. The ten women included in this extraordinary mosaic leave us a heritage that survives the passage of time and the vagaries of fashion. Each one will forever be remembered for something unique, personal, and absolutely inimitable about her image and her every gesture.

We see this in the natural elegance of Audrey Hepburn, her extraordinary timeless class, and the inexhaustible strength of Coco Chanel, who radically changed the image of women, linking a fashion revolution with encouragement for women to carve out a totally new social role.

The explosive sexuality of Marilyn Monroe mixed with a childlike joie de vivre and a tormented, unquenchable desperation. The innate regality of Grace Kelly, and the marvelous and ineluctable Frenchness of Brigitte Bardot, with her love of freedom and independence.

Jackie Kennedy and her extraordinary ability to make herself the center of attention – surely the uncrowned queen of her time, the image of America itself.

Then we have the iconoclasm of Mary Quant, who gave women a new way of looking at their own beauty, along with the fragile, lissome, slender Twiggy, who marked an essential step in the emergence of the modern woman.

Finally, Princess Diana's unique way of interpreting fashion, that incredible capacity to be both humble and regal at the same time.

Each of these women achieved immortality for what they gave to other women.

All were elegant, rebellious spirits, who fully lived out their own lives, in their and our time.

Valeria Manferto De Fabianis

EDITED BY

VALERIA MANFERTO DE FABIANIS

TEXT

PAOLA SALTARI

PREFACE

ANNA MOLINARI

EDITORIAL COORDINATION

GIADA FRANCIA

GIORGIA RAINERI

GRAPHIC DESIGN

MARINELLA DEBERNARDI

Contents

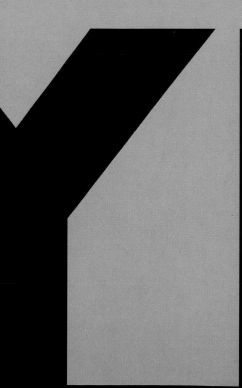

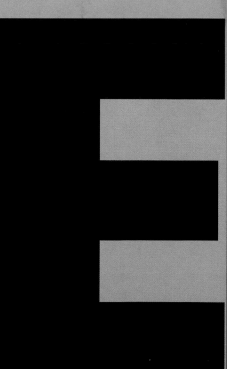

A MATTER OF STYLE

Preface

by Anna Molinari

If we ask ourselves what the objective of every fashion designer is, the answer springs to mind immediately: ideation, creation, trendsetting, innovation; the many fascinating connotations of the word "fashion." the evolution of styles and trends helps defining the history of costume and reflects social dynamics. To "make fashion" is to bring to life creations that can truly be defined as such. Like all artistic interpretation, it entails a complex process of transposing ideas and instincts into something beyond the ephemeral, something that will last. Clothing represents a style, a way of life; it is an art form by virtue of the fact that it is a style.

Today, fashion is a vehicle for designs that everyone will wear and that determine the fundamental criteria for what is beautiful and what is not. The key to the relationship between fashion and society is not the ability to create forms that maintain their raison d'être even while evolving, but rather the expression of what we are, want to be, and will become. Fashion therefore contributes to a collective image associated with emotions, sensations, and universal symbols that give meaning to each of these forms. It is what the icons of beauty presented in this book knew how to achieve, embodying a distinct style ideal that has been imitated by generations of women: the intense courage of Coco Chanel, the independence of Katharine Hepburn, the nonconformity of Lady Diana, the seductiveness of Marilyn, the mischievous ingenuity of BB, the sweet beauty of Audrey Hepburn, the sophisticated beauty of Grace Kelly, the elegance of Jackie Kennedy, the progressivism of Mary Quant, and the bubbly energy of Twiggy. Katharine's androgynous pants, Grace's regal dresses, Audrey's black shift dress and ballet shoes, BB's vichy dress, or the accessories worn by Jackie, have been imitated by all designers. All these women knew how to transform each look into a pure style exercise. Every one of them knew how to uniquely interpret the subtle divide between elegance and style. Elegance can be considered a harmony of proportions, colors, and accessories, achieving femininity and seduction in the balance of these elements. Style is part of one's personality, the outward manifestation of individuality.

I've always believed in a bright and harmonious standard of beauty which is the expression of feminine grace. This is the heart of fashion that must be able to fit modern women who love dreaming above all, and revealing their romantic soul. Icons of style represent the desire for pure beauty to which all women aspire, steeped in an aura of charm and mystery. We may feel like Jackie one day and Audrey another, in a delightful game of role playing and seduction, though i firmly believe that each of us, as women, are uniquely insightful and intriguing, and should be ourselves above all. We should choose and interpret fashion based on our own personalities, like roses, which are the symbol of my collections. Though they express the quintessence of universal beauty, they are different from one an other in scent, colour and shape.

To each her own style…

"FASHIONS CHANGE,
STYLE REMAINS."

•COCO CHANEL•

Introduction

There is a subtle line between fashion and style, two concepts that often tend to be confused. Although they have rather different meanings, one cannot do without the other. Vogue America wrote in September 1976, "Style doesn't depend on fashion. People who have style can accept or ignore fashion. For them fashion is not something to follow but rather to develop, something that they can choose or entirely ignore. Style is spontaneous, a divine gift and it is bestowed upon just a few."

This book is dedicated to ten women who have that gift. Ten leading figures from the 20th century who, over the course of their extraordinary lives, never submitted to fashion but 'made' it, via their choice of dress and more. Style is a very broad category that has more to do with someone's being than her appearance. It is a question of personality, a distinctive feature. The word derives from the Latin *stilus*, a tool used to incise letters onto wax tablets. These women have left so many marks, a large number of which have survived the passage of time. Another essential difference between style and fashion is that the latter is continually in flux, an interminable rush to the new, while style has no sell-by date. To use Coco Chanel's famous motto, "Fashions change, style remains." In 1955, Audrey Hepburn commented that "Everyone has their own style. When we find it, and it's not easy, we should never let it go."

The French stylist who, in the 1920s, 'invented' the modern woman, and the English actress who, according to Richard Avedon, 'invented elegance,' both appear in these pages. Alongside them, we find the other Hepburn, Katharine, who apart from her fame and profession is not related to the actress who played *Sabrina*. Then there are the two most famous, sexy blondes in history, Marilyn Monroe and Brigitte Bardot; the muses of Swinging London, Twiggy and Mary Quant; two princesses of glamour, Grace Kelly and Lady Diana; and, of course, the 'Queen of America,' Jackie Kennedy Onassis.

At this point we won't go into details of individual style or how these ladies still influence what we wear today; we'll cover all that later. However, we would like to highlight how each of these women developed their respective, distinctive image. An image that was so powerful as to imprint itself on millions of others, thus becoming a template – this is what it means to be a *style icon*, a celebrity who exerts an influence on the fashion of her era, representing a source of inspiration for great designers and people in general.

Naturally, fame is an indispensable feature of this process. Style cannot create fashion if it doesn't make itself known. No one managed this better than the early Hollywood studios. They understood how the image of their actors could bestow prestige on a production and create interest in a movie. This is why many of those who we now call style icons were stars of American cinema or were in some way connected with it (even a French symbol like Brigitte Bardot owes her worldwide success to a brief spell in Los Angeles). Up to the 1950s, the big screen was essential in launching new trends, along with fashion magazines. Eventually, television took over, becoming omnipresent. It was no accident that when Jackie Kennedy opened the doors of the White House to CBS and NBC cameras in 1962, she subsequently became the stylistic reference point for an entire generation and many more to follow. This is evidence that the influence exerted by a style icon goes beyond a particular historical moment, the end of a career, or even death.

We only need to read the newspapers to appreciate this. Since Barack Obama won the U.S. presidential election on 4 November 2008, his wife Michelle has been continually compared to Jacqueline Kennedy. The Kennedy Onassis myth also drew in Carla Bruni Sarkozy, France's *première dame* who, on her first official visit to the UK, chose a Dior outfit that was pure Jackie.

Aside from that, if we surf the Web, the *vox populi* of the era of digital communication, we find thousands of fashion sites and blogs in various languages, where girls and young women heap adoration on their idols. These idols often died a long time before they were born. Here are a few of the typical comments we can read about Audrey Hepburn: "I am 12 years old and I think she's very beautiful… my favorite star;" "Refined and sensual in her simplicity, a real icon;" "Unique, incomparable;" "The prototype of perfection." The list could go on forever. The same goes for promotional gifts (t-shirts, calendars, tea cups…) with images of her iconic characters Holly and Sabrina. This (at times debatable) process of commercialization didn't even spare Princess Di, Grace, or BB.

However, the world of fashion has at times tried to raise the tone of its myth-making. Just to mention a few recent episodes, in 2009 Domenico Dolce and Stefano Gabbana designed a tribute-collection to Marilyn Monroe, whose smiling face was printed on wonderful balloon dresses, sheath dresses, and mikado black and white miniskirts. Then, a few months ago, Tommy Hilfiger, a true philosopher of American taste, dedicated his fashion show to Katharine Hepburn and other inspirations from the past, commenting that today, many stars are too "fashion addicted" to be considered style icons.

Indeed, there are conflicting opinions when we think of modern stars who may merit this important but burdensome label. For some it could be Madonna who in her 30-year career in pop music has captured millions of fans, launched many fashions, and inspired stylists of the caliber of Jean-Paul Gaultier. The irrepressible Ms. Ciccone is characterized by her ability to periodically transform herself—her hairstyle, makeup, clothing, even her body, remodeled over the years by vigorous exercise. All this could be described as a chameleonic-style or the absence of a clear style. Whatever it is, we cannot easily compare the singer to yesterday's icons. This is because when we think of Brigitte Bardot (the young one, naturally) we automatically imagine her with wavy disheveled hair, sulky lips and fisherman's pants in Vichy cloth; Twiggy, in our mind, always wears a very short dress, a *gamine* hairstyle and eyelashes plastered with mascara; Mademoiselle Coco wears a cloche and a cascade of pearls around her neck. However, Madonna could morph from a new Evita Peròn, to a Barbie covered with glitter or to the reincarnation of Marilyn Monroe. In essence, these are cultivated references rather than an original manifestation of the artist's (rather strong) personality.

With this in mind, it should be said that someone with the natural instinct that is style is happy to accept the suggestions of professionals like tailors, stylists, make-up artists, but decides herself on how to appear in public. Audrey Hepburn, for example, would never have entered into legend without Givenchy clothes, but it was she who decided on that particular couturier, went to seek him out in Paris and explained to him what she wanted to wear. "My figure really doesn't suit off-the-peg clothes," she admitted in 1966, believing that the Frenchman's creations hid her defects and made her feel more confident. Equally, at the time of her first audition at Metro-Goldwyn-Mayer, the young and still unknown Grace Kelly was already terribly chic. She demanded attention with her pantsuit and white gloves. Then, following a famous row with Joan Crawford about her provocative outfits, Monroe revealed to Modern Screen, "I have to confess that, throughout all my adult life, I have preferred to dress more for men than for women…Each skirt, each dress, each evening gown I chose for their potential effect."

Given the above, we now have to ask a question: did style icons make it through to the new millennium? Certainly there are fashion icons around these days; women who, like the star of *Sex and the City*, Sarah Jessica Parker, are great at keeping up with fast changing fashions. But perhaps there are no more style icons in the classical sense of the term. Of course, stardom itself, without which the icons cannot emerge, is very different nowadays. In 1972, the sociologist Edgar Morin wrote, "Stars are beings that participate in the human and the divine at one and the same time, analogs for certain aspects of heroes of mythology and the gods of Olympus and inspirers of a cult, indeed a type of religion." Almost 40 years later, this definition creaks a little because so-called celebrities are decreasingly divine and indeed evermore earthbound. Now, thanks to the Internet we know everything—or nearly everything—about them. We receive this information in real-time with lots of photographic documentation, which isn't always flattering. To put it another way, there is no longer the indispensible dose of mystery needed to nurse a myth: Marilyn was able to create her reputation as a sex idol in part because we'll never know whether she really slept naked with just two drops of perfume. In the same way we'll never find a picture of Grace Kelly, sweating and her hair messed up after a Pilates lesson.

An aura of being unreachable helps someone become an icon, but it is not enough in itself. Otherwise, it would be impossible to explain the phenomenon of Princess Diana, who following her untimely death became the subject of a sort of beatification. Her fame came from her having changed the way people saw the British crown, not just via her fresh modern look, but also because, with her unaffected manner and resistance to etiquette, she reduced the distance between the royal family and everyone else. In other words, she subverted previous customs. The same goes for all the women celebrated in this volume who, in their own ways, contributed to the process of female emancipation.

Mademoiselle Coco was a shining example of this. Her fashion reflected a world that changed with the end of the First World War and the start of a new era. Elisabeth Weissman in a recent biography of the designer wrote: "the roaring twenties, incarnation of the new woman, dressed and styled by Coco Chanel." She was among the first to embrace the suntan, which had always been seen as a rather inelegant feature of peasant women. She also dared to appear in a bathing costume and to cut her long hair, which she gathered in braids around her head. Chanel did it to break with a model that she judged past its sell-by date, but also to take immediate revenge for the betrayal suffered at the hands of Arthur 'Boy' Capel, the love of her life. Having lost him, she went on to have many lovers, but never married so as to maintain her independence.

This value connects her to Katharine Hepburn, who was born halfway around the world in America, but breathed the same air of sexual equality (her parents, as we'll see, fought for contraception and female suffrage). With her grit and talent, the actress stole the scene (and the trousers!) from her male counterparts, changing the impression that actresses were simply co-stars destined for inferior roles that received lower pay. Indeed, she made history with the contract she signed in 1932 from David O. Selznick's RKO, one of the most powerful producers in Hollywood, who paid her ten times the normal going rate.

Grace Kelly and Jackie Kennedy who seemed to represent a more traditional ideal, in reality tore up the old rulebook. Indeed, both were first ladies in the real sense of the term and not just simply the wives of a prince and a president (it's no coincidence that they loved Chanel's style). In 1961, John F. Kennedy famously quipped, "I am the man who accompanied Jacqueline Kennedy to Paris."

Audrey Hepburn, who nowadays is an emblem of classical elegance, was seen by her contemporaries as a model of rebellion. Everything about her, from the proverbial slimness to the short hair, expressed her rejection of hyper-sexualized femininity—all breasts, hips and flowing tresses—typical of the 1950s, anticipated the slender Mod line of Twiggy and Mary Quant. Even her pumps, explained Rachel Moseley in *Growing Up with Audrey Hepburn*, can be read as a feminist development; no more high heels immobilizing women on a sort of pedestal. Indeed, her flat shoes are an invitation to mobility, action and the freedom to run and dance. This development was also reflected by the high fashion of Givenchy, who invented a chic but uninhibited style, very different from the *New Look* of Dior.

Audrey's image wasn't about sex appeal, but that of Marilyn Monroe and Brigitte Bardot was its apotheosis. And theirs was a very conscious decision. The American star not only posed in the buff for a calendar but also openly talked about nudity. Interviewed by a Hollywood reporter, she said "I dress myself from the feet up. I'm naked and I put on socks and shoes. I wear flesh colored ones because that makes it look as if I'm barefoot." According to her biographer Jenna Glatzer, "Marilyn represented the turning point between the Puritanism of the 1950s and the fashion for 'free love' of the following decade," of which BB was certainly an icon. This was not just for her movies, where she didn't seem to have any qualms about stripping off her clothes. It was also because after having married her Pygmalion, Roger Vadim, while still an adolescent, she married three more times and had an infinite series of famous relationships. We can't forget that *Je t'aime, moi non plus*, the movie that provoked a scandal in 1969 for its overt eroticism, was written for her by Serge Gainsbourg (even though she appeared in it along with Jane Birkin).

In those same years, across the Channel in Swinging London, Mary Quant dressed the youth revolution with her instant fashion and the miniskirt—which became an icon of the final liberation of femininity. Like the symbolic miniskirt, Twiggy, the skinny model, with whom an entire generation of girls identified, just wanted to enjoy herself.

In talking about these exceptional women who changed fashion and were pioneers of style, we gain a slightly better insight into our cultural history. As Oscar Wilde argued, "Only superficial people don't judge on appearances. The real mystery of the world is the visible, not the invisible."

1 Audrey Hepburn in the unforgettable *Sabrina* (1954).
2 Grace Kelly in Côte d'Azur style, in the film *To Catch a Thief* (1955).

3 Katharine Hepburn in *The Rainmaker* (1956).
8 Grace Kelly and Audrey Hepburn at the 28th Oscar ceremony.

16 Marilyn Monroe smiles on a break wearing nothing but a robe.
17 Twiggy, in 1966, the year photographer Barry Lategan launched her career.

COCO
CHANEL

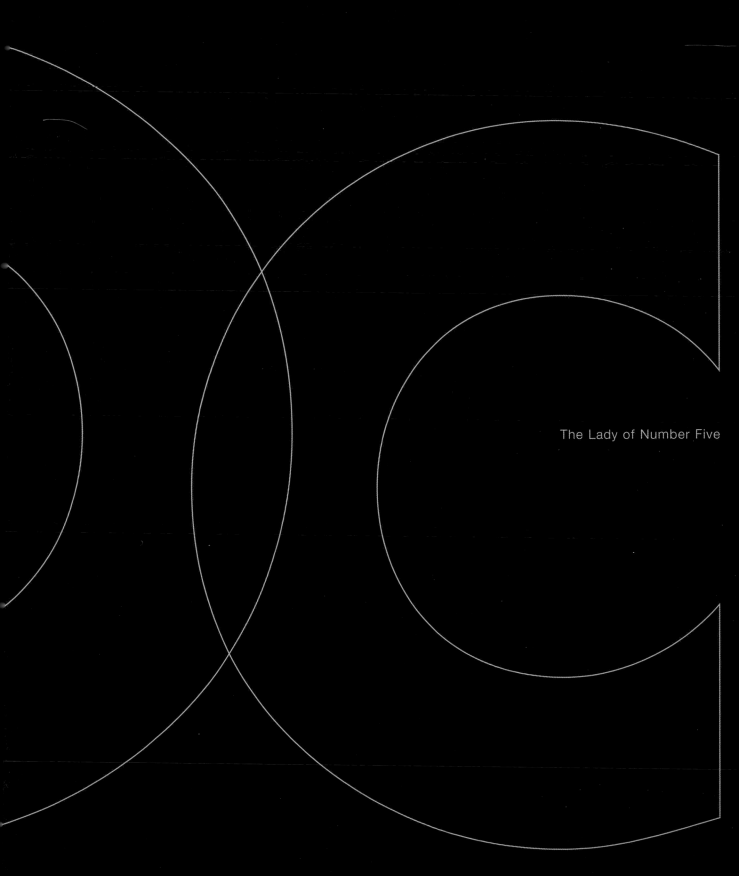

The Lady of Number Five

«A WOMAN
IS ALWAYS
OVERDRESSED
AND INSUFFICIENTLY
ELEGANT.»

•COCO CHANEL•

In 1973, the semiotician Roland Barthes wrote that "Chanel keeps fashion away from barbarism and replenishes it with all the classical values: reason, naturalness, durability, and joy at giving pleasure not shock." The world's greatest ever stylist would have appreciated that comment, given her belief that "fashion is made to become unfashionable." Unfortunately, she died two years earlier, at nearly 90 years old, after a life that was as intense and extraordinary as the heritage she left to us. Without Gabrielle 'Coco' Chanel, we wouldn't have the black sheath dress, N°5 perfume, the tweed pantsuit, the jewels, the two-tone shoes, and many other classics, which may very well last for centuries. All this was quite an achievement for someone who hadn't studied design, who learned how to sew in an orphanage, and who as a girl tried to launch a career in cabaret in Provence, in southern France. It was here she picked up her iconic nickname, Coco. This nickname served to remind her of a sad and seedy past, best forgotten or at least embellished with a bit of fiction.

The ambitious Chanel took as her motto: "If you were born without wings, do nothing to prevent them from growing." With the assistance of two rich and powerful partners, Étienne Balsan and Arthur 'Boy' Capels, she had three boutiques by 1915. One was in Deauville, one in Biarritz and another in Paris, on Rue Cambon, which is still the headquarters of the Chanel house. By 1919, at 36 years of age, she reigned over the most powerful economic empire ever built by a woman. It all began with a straw hat, designed by accident but so original that it grabbed the attention of a famous actress of the era and started a sensation. Indeed, Coco's creation bore no relation to the headgear in fashion at the time, festooned with feathers, veils, and bows. She removed all excess, sketching out the basis of a new concept of luxury: purity and essentiality, because "nothing is so stupid as to confuse simplicity with poverty."

Her clothing was proof of this; she was always inspired by her environment. For example, in 1913, observing the jersey worn by a Norman fisherman, she launched the marinière: a t-shirt with white and blue stripes that became the summer 'uniform' of women on holiday in the exclusive seaside resort of Deauville. But Mademoiselle (as her workers called her) also understood how to meet the needs of other customers. She catered to the wives, daughters, and sisters, who took the reins of the family businesses while their men were away at the front during the First World War. Although they were working, they still wanted to feel beautiful and elegant. Coco commented, "I gave women's bodies their freedom back; their bodies sweated under their corsets, their underwear, their padding." She shortened dresses and did away with bustiers and thus gave birth to the 'modern woman.' This woman didn't need to be assisted by a man as she struggled to walk with yards of fabric clawing at her legs. She needed no maids to help close the hundreds of hooks on her corset.

The icon of a new emancipated femininity, Mademoiselle was one of the first to wear her hair short, it was wavy and frequently under a cloche, the bell-shaped hat that was all the rage in the 1920s. Coco's revolution introduced trousers and flowing dresses without waists, with short sleeves even for daywear. Above all, she brought us jersey wool, a material that had only previously been used for lingerie. This discovery was born of necessity (silk, cotton, and precious wool were in scarce supply due to the war) but it was brilliant. She used jersey wool to make dresses but also loose pullovers, cardigans and the first famous pantsuits. Coco went for sober colors: beige, sand, and navy, with dashes of white and Bordeaux in the men's cut satin pajamas—which she loved. She was also the first person to produce women's fashion in black; a color no one wanted to wear, even in the evening, as it was the color of mourning. Inspired by the uniforms of female office workers, in 1926, she created a masterpiece: the *petite robe noire*, or the little black dress. A crêpe de chine sheath dress with tight-fitting sleeves and pouching on the sides, suitable for any occasion. Rigorous, it had a single necklace, a long string of (preferably fake) pearls. Costume jewelry was another of Chanel's happy discoveries. She came up with maxi-necklaces to be worn in profusion with earrings, solid bracelets and broaches shaped like camellias, her favorite flower, which became the symbol of the fashion house along with the double 'C' logo.

In 1921, she launched the perfume par excellence, N°5. After almost a century, it is still the world's best selling fragrance. Created by chemist Ernest Beaux, it represented a breakthrough for at least three reasons: it was the first time that natural and synthetic essences had been mixed; the name (which derives from it being the fifth bottle proposed by Beaux) is light years away from the various *Nuits de Chine* and *Désir Princier* in circulation at the time; and the bottle, a simple parallelepiped, broke with Art Nouveau style. It was so successful that five became Coco's lucky number.

It is no coincidence that the symbol of her revival, after the dark years and the closure of her studio between 1939 and 1954, was the 2.55, the first shoulder bag named after its date of birth (February 1955). "Tired of carrying my handbags and losing them, I added a strap and put it on my shoulder," she commented on this cult object, made out of leather or topstitched *matelassé* (quilted) material. With its gold chain, the 2.55 became the fetish of Chanel's 'new woman' whose wardrobe included tweed pantsuits with a collarless jacket embellished with jewel-buttons and piped in a contrasting color, a lined silk blouse, and a pair of two-color pumps with a cream upper and black toe, designed to make the feet look smaller, rounded off the outfit. At over 70 years old, Coco performed what *Life* magazine called another 'revolution.' She invented a simple but impeccable figure in opposition to Dior's *New Look* that, with whalebones, girdles and balloon dresses, brought back the sexy side of femininity, but also the specter of submission against which Chanel always fought. Her victory can be seen in the number of imitators ("My greatest reward is to be constantly picked at by forty thousand couturiers"), but her consecration came in the 1970s when her clothes became the uniform of the latest generation of jet-setting women, the young, attractive, fashionable, fawned on by the press and television. Does that bring anyone in particular to mind? Jackie Kennedy, of course.

25 Mademoiselle with one of her famous jackets in 1937, the year she charmed Luchino Visconti.

26 Gabrielle in 1936, pictured among her Coromandel screen, acquired at the time of her relationship with Boy Capel.

27 Coco poses for Roger Schall in 1938, in a beret and striped men's cut vest.

28-29 and 29 An essential element of the Chanel style was costume jewelry, or fake jewelry, a fashion Coco launched in the '20s. Her first collection of fine jewelry, all platinum and diamonds, was presented on wax mannequins in 1932.

30 Coco smiles at the camera in 1936. Her nickname comes from a popular French song that the dressmaker was particularly fond of, called "Who's Seen Coco in the Trocadero?"

33 Gabrielle in the mid-1960s, pictured in her luxurious Parisian apartment. Contrary to her aristocratic image, she was the daughter of a domestic servant and a small time salesman.

«Fashion always reflects the times we live in, even though, when times are dull, we prefer to forget them.»

•Coco Chanel•

«I love luxury. And luxury lies not in richness and ornateness but in the absence of vulgarity. Vulgarity is the ugliest word in our language. I stay in the game to fight it.»

•Coco Chanel•

34 and 35 Mademoiselle at work in the late '50s. Above, she puts the finishing touches on a cocktail dress. On the right, she observes Marie-Hélène Arnaud, her star model.

36-37 Two legends side by side: Coco and Romy Schneider in 1960, where she sports one of her legendary tweed suits with a contrasting profile, to this day a symbol of the fashion house. Mademoiselle, who didn't know how to draw, developed the clothing based on the client, modeling it on the movements of her body.

38-39 Mademoiselle in 1969, with one of her beloved cloche hats. The designer stated, "I would never give up hats or fur. What kind of woman would I be?"

40 and 41 Two relaxing moments for Gabrielle Chanel in 1964: at the age of 81, she's still impeccably dressed in her women's suit, with a string of pearls and that unforgettable cigarette.

42 Coco descends the staircase lined with mirrors that dominate her Parisian atelier. This is where she watched in terror as the show that marked her return to fashion took place on February 5, 1954.

43 Whether working or taking a stroll, Gabrielle is sure to be elegant, because she never forgets to "be a symbol of style for the whole world."

45 Coco arrives at her fashion house headquarters at Rue Cambon 31 in Paris, as she did every morning. Perhaps it was no coincidence that she died on a Sunday (January 10, 1971), a day she detested because it wasn't a workday.

«NOTHING IS SO STUPID
AS TO CONFUSE
SIMPLICITY
WITH POVERTY.»

•COCO CHANEL•

KATHARINE
HEPBURN

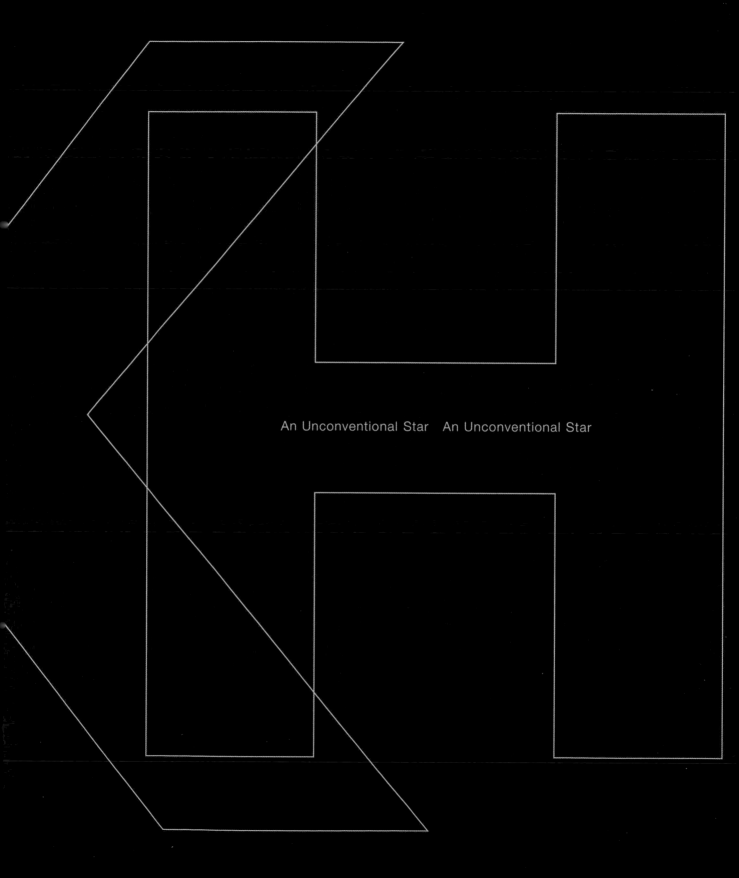

An Unconventional Star   An Unconventional Star

«THERE ARE WOMEN AND WOMEN—AND THEN THERE'S KATE. THERE ARE ACTRESSES AND ACTRESSES—AND THEN THERE'S HEPBURN.»

•FRANK CAPRA•

Perhaps no one has managed to better encapsulate Katharine Hepburn's uniqueness. Beautiful, although light-years away from the stereotype of a sex kitten, she was elegant, but too sophisticated to be to everyone's taste. During her long life (she died on 29 August 2003 at 96 years old), she fought against the cliché of a star as being all parties and glitz, presenting a totally different idea of the feminine. This included her look. Off set she never used make-up, jewelry or perfume. However, with her snobbish non-conformity, the first woman in Hollywood to wear trousers was the biggest diva of the lot. She was also, almost by accident, one of the most glamorous. She maintained: "I always dress in the same way so I don't have to think: 'What to wear?'" without imagining that, in 1986, she would receive a prize from the Council of Fashion Designers of America for her influence on 20th century fashion. However, these weren't they type of awards that interested her.

In a career spanning over sixty years, she appeared in 48 movies and collected 12 Oscar nominations for best actress, winning for her performances in *Morning Glory* (1932), *Guess Who's Coming to Dinner?* (1967), *The Lion in Winter* (1968) and *On Golden Pond* (1981). This record remains unequalled, like that of never having personally collected a statuette. It was inconceivable for someone too private even to go to a restaurant to participate in an Oscar ceremony, with the red carpets, flash photography and all the rest. And, of course, she didn't even have a single evening dress in her wardrobe—or actually any female clothing at all. In 2004, all of her personal belongings were put up for auction at Sotheby's. Among paintings, photographs, furnishings and other reminders of her incredible life, there was just a single dress. The cream velvet one she wore in 1928 when she married Ludlow Ogden Smith, the businessman she divorced just six years later.

It is well known that she was idiosyncratic about dresses. "When I hear a man say that he prefers women in dresses, I tell him: 'Try it, put one on'," she declared in a 1993 television autobiography. It seems that this rejection, dating back to the 1930s, owed its origin to the garter-belt; the actress couldn't stand them and decided to wear socks instead, inventing an androgynous style she made famous and that has been so widely imitated. To gain an idea of what we are talking about, we could just watch two of her best movies, *The Philadelphia Story* (1940) and *Woman of the Year* (1942), in which she was free to express her taste in clothes (a small curiosity: Adrian, the designer of *The Wizard of Oz* (1939), was the costume designer in both productions and this is no chance occurrence as he is considered the inspiration for the other pioneer of menswear, Greta Garbo).

Katharine-style trousers are wide, pleated, turned-up and high waisted. They are worn with socks and flat lace-

48 **The actress relaxing in Connecticut, in July 1957. Her 'uniform' off the set was a men's shirt and wide-legged pants.**

50 **Hepburn behind the camera while shooting *Guess Who's Coming to Dinner* (1967), the last film she made with the well-loved Spencer Tracy.**

up shoes. She also wore a men's shirt, preferably a button-down with the collar fastened by two small buttons. An impeccably cut single-breasted jacket with slightly padded shoulders rounded off the look. The colors were always sober (white, black, and beige) and the fabrics always tough, with a preference for gabardine and tweed. But velvet also got a look, used for example, for a smoking jacket that Hepburn wore in a scene from *Woman of the Year*. It was very chic, 20 years before the historic collection in which Yves Saint Laurent invented the women's tuxedo. One consequence of this has been the fashion trade's work in adapting the staples of male fashion to the female form. Naturally, in her case the clothes were all made-to-measure. It is really for this reason that she never looks like a cross dresser. Rather, our view is different from the one held when she made her screen debut in 1932, when trousers were not just considered unsuitable for women but actually immoral.

In an era when the Hollywood ideal was sweet and gushing, essentially submitted to the opposite sex, Kate arrived like a tidal wave. Above all she was physically different; she stood 5'6" (168cm), which was tall compared to other starlets of the time – Marilyn Monroe, who began her career as a model in the 1940s, measured just 5'4" (163cm). Her body was lean and muscled, forged by the sports she played throughout her life, including tennis, golf and swimming. Every day she did twenty lengths of an unheated pool; a practice that enabled her to, at the advanced age of 74, personally perform the unforgettable scene in which she saves Henry Fonda from the freezing waters in *On Golden Pond*.

It's also worth noting that when she was a young child, she called herself 'Jimmy' and wore her natural red hair cut very short, despite how we all remember her from movies – with her distinctive wavy, disheveled hair. Her mannish behavior irritated studio managers, who once took her jeans and gym shoes (another detail of her avant-garde style) from the changing room during a screen test. Even Spencer Tracy, the only great love of her life besides acting, was prejudiced against her: "How can I work with a woman who has dirty nails, dresses like a man and who is probably a lesbian?" However, he only had to see her on set to change his mind, and thus began the most romantic and famous extramarital affair in Hollywood; 25 years together, even though the devoutly Catholic Tracy never wanted to divorce his wife. To be 'the other woman' without fearing people's judgment was another sign of Katharine's uniqueness, gleaned from an upbringing in a very open upper middle class environment with no taboos. She was born in Hartford, Connecticut on 12 May 1907. Her father, Thomas, was a urologist and strong public advocate of contraception; her mother, Katharine Martha Houghton, was a suffragette who fought for abortion rights. Without these details we cannot hope to really understand 'The First Lady of Cinema.'

53 *Woman of the Year*, from 1942, is a film that defines Kate's refined, androgynous style.

Here she's impeccably dressed in a black blazer with slightly padded shoulders.

54 and 55 The leading lady rehearses for George Bernard Shaw's *The Millionairess* at the Apollo Theater in London, in 1952. White knee socks are just visible under her beige pants, worn with loafers.

The actress had a well-known aversion to garter belts.

56 The actress playing baseball on May 25, 1952. Hepburn was a real health nut: she didn't drink, she went to bed early, and she got up at 4:30 am to swim in an unheated pool.

57 Kate was born in Hartford, Connecticut on May 12, 1907. She returned whenever possible, taking long bike rides and replacing her pants with shorts, which showed off her long legs

and scandalized the neighbors.

58-59 In 1935, Kate plays the title character in *Sylvia Scarlett*, who dresses as a man to evade the police

60 and 61 Katharine on a staircase, waiting to film a scene from the Sidney Lumet drama, *Long Day's Journey Into Night* (1956). She liked shirts with button-down collars, and her preferred colors were black, white, and neutral tones.

62 and 63 The star arriving in London to bring *The Millionairess* to the stage. Katharine wears a complete suit with a two-button jacket over a cardigan and a white turtleneck. The two-tone oxfords on her feet were custom-made, like the majority of her wardrobe. Interestingly, Hepburn played another great "rebel" on Broadway in 1969: Coco Chanel.

64 and 65 The actress on the set of *Long Day's Journey Into Night* (1956). Katharine was a natural redhead and wore her wavy hair down throughout the '40s, after which it was always up in a loose chignon. She wore no makeup or perfume off set, showing her heavily freckled skin.

67 Katharine Hepburn in the movie *The Rainmaker* (1956). Despite her masculine appearance, this diva was a real lady. As Sidney Poitier recalled, "At the end of each film she wrote letters to everyone in the crew and gave out handmade gifts."

«I think every actress in the world looked up to her with a kind of reverence and a sense of, 'Oh boy, if only I could be like her.' We never looked at her with envy or jealousy because she worked with such grace and wit and charm.»

•Elizabeth Taylor•

MARILYN
MONROE

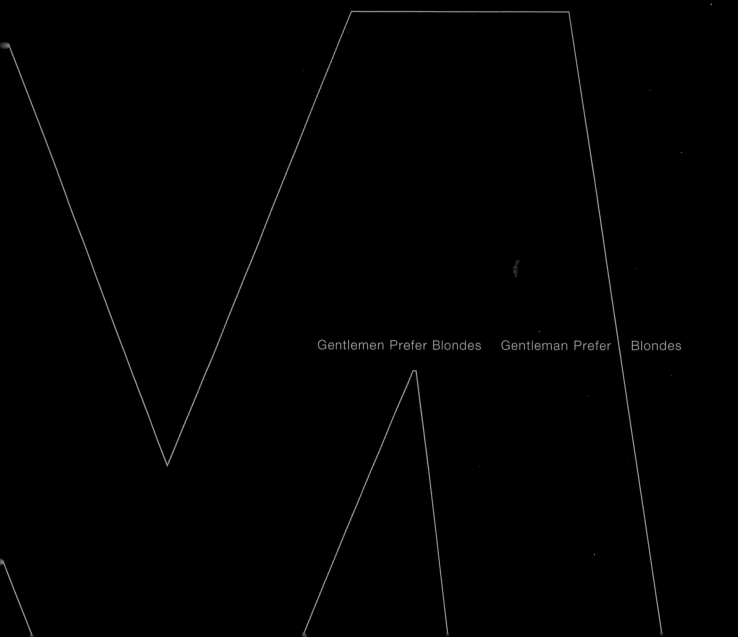

Gentlemen Prefer Blondes   Gentleman Prefer   Blondes

«I MOSTLY DAYDREAMED
ABOUT BEAUTY. I DREAMED
OF BEING SO BEAUTIFUL THAT
PEOPLES' HEADS WOULD TURN
WHEN I WALKED BY.»

•MARILYN MONROE•

In 1999, when *People* magazine picked the sexiest woman of the 20th century, no one on the editorial team had the slightest hesitation: the title belonged to Marilyn Monroe. Whatever some may think of her as an artist, there's no denying that the woman who played Sugar Kane in *Some Like It Hot* (1959) was far more than a beautiful and provocative post-war actress. Monroe is as much a part of our culture as the famous portrait of her by Andy Warhol. She is a piece of history and possibly the most beloved, envied and famous woman of all times.

What's her secret? "She was a paradoxical mixture between the angelic and the seductive, domination and submission. She loved to laugh, although she was very sad," wrote Jenna Glatzer in her illustrated biography. Many have tried and still try to match her; most notably Madonna, who to some degree owes her status as a pop icon to the late movie star. The 1985 music video for "Material Girl" is an explicit homage to the Howard Hawks movie *Gentlemen Prefer Blondes* (1953). In the film, Monroe sings "Diamonds Are a Girl's Best Friend" while dripping with jewels and clad in a pink satin bustier dress, designed by William "Billy" Travilla. She was immortalized in this image, although it only revealed a fraction of her true personality. Yes, she was glamorous and exquisite, but also far more intelligent and sensitive than Hollywood wanted us to believe.

In many ways Marilyn Monroe was more a celebrity than a person; the name itself was dreamed up in 1946. When the future star of *Niagara* (1953) and *River of No Return* (1954) was born on 1 June 1926 in Los Angeles, she was named Norma Jeane Mortenson. That didn't last long as her mother, Gladys, subsequently baptized her Norma Jeane Baker, after her first husband. The mysterious surnames and suspected fathers (Monroe believed her real father was Charles Stanley Gifford) were just the beginning, her life played out like a movie script—but one very different from the light-hearted comedies that made her famous.

Growing up, Norma Jeane's head was filled with the idea of Hollywood, cinema and the stars of the era. But her childhood was spent shuttling between guardians and foster homes, often filled with violence, as the severely mentally ill Gladys abandoned her after birth. Perhaps this is where her desire for stardom and public acclaim came from. Her opportunity arose in 1945, when 16-year-old Norma Jeane, already married to James Dougherty, was spotted by photographer David Conover while she was working in a munitions factory. She was not just beautiful, but magnetic and completely uninhibited in front of the camera. In the space of just a few months, she become a well-known model and the following year signed her first contract with 20th Century Fox, where Ben Lyon advised her to call herself Marilyn, a name that paired well with her mother's maiden name of Monroe.

70 Monroe in *The Seven Year Itch* (1955). The legendary dress is by William Travilla.

72 Marilyn wearing a high-necked pinstripe dress and wedge sandals with no socks, photographed in 1954.

Her personal life played out in the public eye: the divorce from James, the sexy *Miss Golden Dreams* calendar with the picture that Hugh Hefner subsequently bought for the first edition of Playboy, the cover of Life, the elopement with baseball champion Jo DiMaggio in 1954, her third husband, playwright Arthur Miller, two abortions, and 31 films—of which the last (*Something's Got to Give*) remained uncompleted at the time of her premature death on 5 August 1962, due to an overdose of barbiturates. It was a tragic end still shrouded in mystery—was it suicide, a fatal accident, or was it murder, due to her relationship with the Kennedy brothers? It all fueled Monroe's reputation as a sex symbol.

Her hair was one of her most powerful tools of seduction: shiny, silky, always perfectly cut and wavy, and very blonde. There is no doubt that Norma Jeane would have been so successful if she had stayed her natural reddish-brown. The world's most infamous blonde became so at 19 years old, when Emmeline Snively, director of the Blue Book Modeling Agency, suggested she have a perm to 'contain' her thick curls and that she should bleach her hair. Apparently, she tried nine different shades before settling upon the platinum that passed into history as 'Marilyn blonde.' "I am against excessive tanning. I like to be blonde all over," she told *Pageant* magazine, talking about her milky white skin, which she moisturized with tubs of Nivea. The secret of her shiny face was something else however—she used Vaseline rather than cream. Her timeless make-up was much more interesting: black eyeliner and lots of mascara to emphasize her gaze, well-defined eyebrows, and blood red lips.

"I don't know who invented high heels but all men owe him a lot," commented the star, who stressed how a sensual walk is key to the 'construction' of a sex symbol. She was a real mistress of the slinky walk. It is also rumored that she had one shoe heel lowered by a centimeter to increase her wiggle. And it was shoes—her favorites were peep-toe pumps and Plexiglas platforms—around which her outfits were based. For clothing, she only selected items that made her appear unequivocally feminine, like the siren dress by Jean Louis which she wore during her performance at President Kennedy's 45th birthday party. It was powder pink, festooned with two thousand crystal beads and so close-fitting that it had to be sewn on her. The effect was so unforgettable that the dress sold for over one million dollars in 1999. However, the most replicated dress ever is the white, silk-crepe, halter-neck dress with accordion pleated skirt from the metro scene in *The Seven Year Itch*. It was designed by the aforementioned Travilla, Marilyn's favorite designer both on and off set. Whatever she wore, she was a star; even when it was a simple pullover (with no bra underneath!) matched with a tubular skirt or when she mischievously mentioned that she slept naked, wearing only two drops of Chanel *N°5*. "Bye Bye Baby."

75 The actress appears at the Ambassador Hotel in New York wearing a white dress: one of her favorite colors, along with black and red.

76-77 Despite her predilection for skimpy clothing, Marilyn was not opposed to wearing men's shirts with jeans or pencil skirts off set. Like at the civil ceremony where she wed her third husband, Arthur Miller, on June 29, 1956.

78 Marilyn in 1950, wearing her star 'uniform': a form-fitting pullover, below-the-knee pencil skirt, high-heeled pumps and dark glasses.

79 The actress had a passion for furs, which she frequently wore. She's surprised with a sable, a gift from Joe DiMaggio, on a summer afternoon in 1953. Below, however, she is nude.

80 and 81 The diva in a low-necked dress. Bloomingdale's in Beverly Hills was her favorite place to shop.

83 Touching up her lips on the set of *Clash By Night* (1952). The diva frequently asked the makeup artists to redo her makeup.

84-85 The sensual Monroe is barefoot in a black satin slip, photographed by Inge Morath on the set of her last film, *The Misfits*, in 1961.

«If I wear a girdle it will flatten me. Tell me why I should want to be flattened!»

·Marilyn Monroe·

86-87 Marilyn in 1954, surrounded by dozens of Korean photographers, ready to snap pictures of the star as she visits the American troops stationed in the country.

88 and 89 The diva blows kisses to her fans, who remain numerous to this day. Madonna and Scarlett Johansson are among the stars who have tried to emulate her style.

91 Marilyn involuntarily became the biggest celebrity endorser of Chanel *N°5*, which she often declared her favorite perfume.   ·

«I'VE ALWAYS FELT
AT EASE WHEN
I LOOKED
UNEQUIVOCALLY
FEMININE.»

•MARILYN MONROE•

92-93 Marilyn shows off for the American Army in Korea, in February 1954. In spite of the freezing cold, she wears a black lamé dress with spaghetti straps. She would later say, "Singing for those soldiers was the highest point in my life."

MARILYN MONROE

Gentlemen Prefer Blondes

94-95 The actress on the set of *The Seven Year Itch* (1955). In 1958, her legendary hair would be entrusted to the care of Kenneth Battelle, Jackie Kennedy's hairdresser.

96 Marilyn knew she was seductive, even in a black turtleneck. After her death in 1962, Joe DiMaggio placed a bouquet of roses on her tomb three days a week, for twenty years.

«Being a sex symbol
is a burden, especially
when I feel tired,
hurt and confused.»

•Marilyn Monroe•

AUDREY
HEPBURN

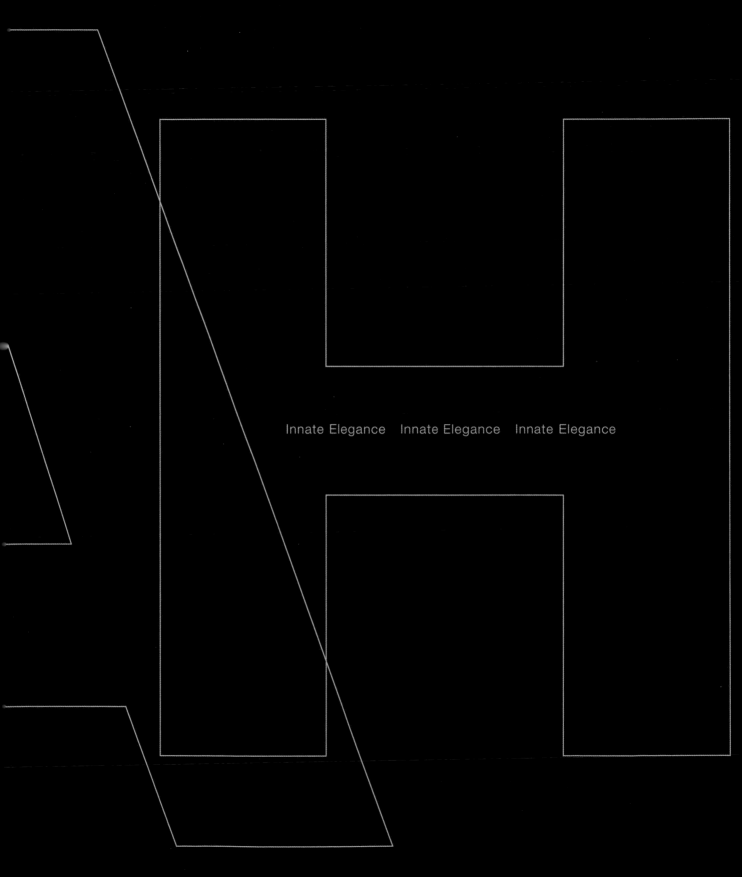

Innate Elegance   Innate Elegance   Innate Elegance

«I DON'T NEED A BEDROOM
TO PROVE MY WOMANLINESS.
I CAN CONVEY JUST AS MUCH
APPEAL FULLY CLOTHED, PICKING
APPLES OFF A TREE OR STANDING
IN THE RAIN».

·AUDREY HEPBURN·

It is said that one evening, just before an event, Audrey Hepburn spilled coffee on her dress. Not having a spare, she borrowed a white shirt from her husband Mel Ferrer. She knotted the shirttails at the waist, rolled up the sleeves, turned up the collar and paired it with a flared skirt. She went to the event never imagining that a few days later scores of young women would imitate her last minute wardrobe change. Perhaps the story is apocryphal, but it is certain that few actresses had as much influence on the fashion of the fifties and sixties as Audrey Hepburn. And it's felt today as the items she popularized are still considered essential to every woman's wardrobe.

"Today women take for granted the things they wear, but if it hadn't been for Audrey Hepburn they would-n't even be wearing them," declared stylist Michael Kors in 1993, a few days after the death of the English ac-tress. Hepburn is synonymous with several classic styles including smoking pants, launched by *Sabrina* and seen again in *Funny Face*, the trench coat made legendary by the kiss between Holly and Paul in the final scene of *Breakfast at Tiffany's*, and the giant white sunglasses she sported in *How to Steal a Million*.

"She could have been a designer; she had perfect taste," wrote Edith Head, Hollywood's most successful costume designer, illustrating that Hepburn's style was very much her own. She was not just beautiful, but pos-sessed the grace of someone who studied dance from a young age and, above all, the elegance of down-at-heel aristocracy (daughter of Dutch baroness Ella van Heemstra and British diplomat Joseph Hepburn Rush-ton). Her elegance was apparent in William Wyler's 1953 movie *Roman Holiday*, a performance that earned her an Oscar at the tender age of twenty-four. She wore a close fitting blouse, silk scarf around her neck, and a full, cotton skirt belted at the waist in the scene where Princess Anna, in rebellion against protocol and her elegant dresses, escapes on a Vespa with Gregory Peck to tour the world. The merit for this goes not just to Head's costumes, a reworking of the casual new look invented by Dior in 1947, but to Hepburn, who incarnated a new, modern model of femininity opposed to the shapely sexiness in vogue in Hollywood at the time.

"Before her appearance on the scene, the rules of elegance dictated that girls were to imitate older women. Youth was an embarrassing transitional phase," wrote Scott Brizel in *Audrey Hepburn: International Cover Girl*. "By chance, she followed Richard Avedon's advice to emphasize and not hide her distinctive traits." Those traits include the body of an eternal adolescent without curvy hips or ample breasts, ten years before the phenome-non of the skinny model; a soap and water face centered on doe-eyes, popularized by the Italian Alberto De Rossi; thick eyebrows; and her natural brown hair, cut short.

100   Audrey's all-white Givenchy look in *How to Steal a Million* (1966).

102 In *Sabrina* (1954), Audrey wears her first Givenchy evening gown, known as the Inez de Castro.

That in itself was not new; Louise Brooks launched the *à la garçon* style in the 1920s. However, Hepburn's hairstyle in *Roman Holiday*, designed by Grazia De Rossi (the wife of Alberto), was more impish and easy to imitate.

This was also the case for the entire wardrobe of *Sabrina* (1954), her second Hollywood movie and first collaboration with Hubert de Givenchy, the young French designer who invented minimal fashion – a very clean, essential but sophisticated form of high fashion. His name doesn't appear in the closing titles of the Billy Wilder movie, because he didn't have the time to design anything original for the production. However, we know that Hepburn personally chose his extraordinary garments after visiting the tailor's Parisian showroom. Unforgettable ensembles from the film include the bustier dress in white organdy with beaded pearl floral stitch-work. But there was also the cocktail dress with boat neck that has since been known as *décolleté Sabrina*. The Hepburn-Givenchy pairing is also indelibly associated with the sheath dress. The straight black dress was invented by Coco Chanel in 1926 but consecrated in 1961 by the Blake Edwards' romantic comedy *Breakfast at Tiffany's*, in which Hepburn plays socialite and gold digger, Holly Golightly. The couturier designed her two sleeveless versions of the *little black dress* or *petit noir*: the short model in cloqué silk with a slightly flared frilly skirt, combined with a big wide-brimmed hat. And the so-called 'work clothes,' an evening gown, narrow at the waist and with a magnificent low-cut back paired with long, black gloves. The impact of the film on the collective imagination was such that in a survey published in 2007 by the United Kingdom's *Daily Mail*, the sheath dress was voted the most important garment in the history of clothing, ahead of jeans and the Wonderbra.

Under the guise of Holly Golightly, Hepburn launched a variety of fashions, including the bouffant, hair gathered and backcombed, designed by Grazia De Rossi; and the maxi necklace, multiple strings of pearls worn together. And, of course, the tiara – although off set "Miss Tiffany" only wore a ring and a pair of diamond earrings. Her shoes in the film were favored by dancers of the era and are still popular today among the young (and not so young) who are probably ignorant of the fact that Salvatore Ferragamo invented them for Hepburn at the time of *Roman Holiday*. As Paola Jacobbi wrote in her book, *I Want Those Shoes!*, Hollywood's beloved Italian shoemaker was inspired by Hepburn's past as a dancer and by her height (over 5'5"/165cm) to create low-heeled walking shoes based on dance shoes. She didn't need high heels to be attractive, as Ralph Lauren commented in 1990: "*There are two or three people who the public will never forget for their charm and elegance. Audrey Hepburn is number one.*"

«[IN FILM] THERE HAD BEEN
THIS REAL DROUGHT,
WHEN ALONG CAME CLASS.»

•BILLY WILDER•

110 and 110-111 The "work clothes" are another legendary Givenchy look for *Breakfast at Tiffany's* (1961): a long silk dress with a low back, matching gloves, strands of pearls, and a cigarette holder. The sequence in front of the Tiffany's window shows off Hepburn's "new" hairstyle: an upsweep with highlights.

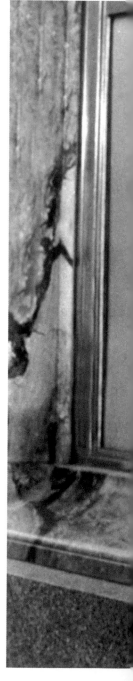

112 The lampshade hat and sunglasses reminiscent of the Ray-Ban Wayfarer model are among the Givenchy accessories for *Breakfast at Tiffany's* (1961).

113 Sabrina wears the Glen Cove Givenchy suit, made of gray oxford, in the scene at the station. A turban and drop earrings complete the ensemble.

113

114-115 Audrey sports a casual version of the New Look in *Roman Holiday* (1953). Costume designer Edith Head used limp fabric to make her look less chic.

117 The main character in *Funny Face* (1957), the musical with Fred Astaire about the world of fashion, wears a blouse and shantung cigarette pants with a fitted waist.

118 and 119 Hepburn's experience as a dancer came through in this look from *Sabrina* (1954): fitted pullover, capri pants and Salvatore Ferragamo ballet flats.

120-121 After dedicating the later years of her life to UNICEF (The United Nations Children's Fund), the leading lady passed away on January 20, 1993. She was born in Brussels, Belgium on May 4, 1929.

«GIVENCHY DRESSES ARE
SO BEAUTIFUL AND SIMPLE,
I FELT WONDERFUL
IN THEM.»

·AUDREY HEPBURN·

«SHE HAD A NATURAL GRACE,
AN INNATE ELEGANCE,
A DAZZLING SPLENDOR.»

•CECIL BEATON•

GRACE
KELLY

Fire and Ice   Fire and Ice

«I'VE BEEN ACCUSED OF BEING
COLD, SNOBBISH, DISTANT.
THOSE WHO KNOW ME
WELL KNOW THAT I'M NOTHING
OF THE SORT. IF ANYTHING, THE
OPPOSITE IS TRUE.»

·GRACE KELLY·

Grace Kelly was aware of the image that the world had of her. She knew she was able to provoke both love and hatred. That apart she was nigh perfect. Her milky skin, blond hair, blue eyes, and slender willowy figure, made for an uncommon beauty. However, what rendered her unreachable above all was her class, that innate capacity to appear pristine and flawless on any occasion. Grace Kelly's natural elegance is still one of her unforgettable traits even today, almost thirty years after her premature death in a tragic road accident in 1982. Of course, this event did nothing to tarnish the legend of the Hollywood star who left cinema at the peak of her success for the love of a prince. People still write books about her. The princess's extraordinary wardrobe has been displayed at major cultural institutions (including London's Victoria and Albert Museum). Women of every country and class still consider her a role model. That includes heiress Ivanka Trump, who asked designer Vera Wang to design a dress in 'Grace Kelly style' for her 1989 wedding. It cost 30 thousand dollars. But what exactly is the 'Grace Kelly style?' To understand we need to take a step back and acknowledge that first and foremost she was Her Royal Highness the Princess of Monaco.

Grace Patricia Kelly was born on 12 November 1929 into an upper middle class family in Philadelphia. Her father, John Brendan, a former manual laborer of Irish heritage, made his fortune from a brick factory. Her uncle George was an actor and playwright, who won a Pulitzer Prize. It was he who transmitted a love of the stage to Grace who, in 1947, was admitted to the American Academy of Dramatic Art in New York. In 1951, after debuting as a model and on television, she won a small part in *Fourteen Hours* by Henry Hathaway. The following year, she played lead in the western *High Noon* alongside Gary Cooper. However, Alfred Hitchcock was essential to her career, directing her in three memorable movies: the demonic *Dial M for Murder* and the intriguing *Rear Window*, both in 1954; and the detective comedy *To Catch a Thief*, in 1955, prophetically set on the Cote d'Azur. Talking about his muse, the great master of suspense said: "She is seductive without being sexy. Under an icy surface, she seems to burn with an inner fire that will do wonders on the screen."

Her strong personality is what made Grace Kelly unique. On screen it simply shined. She chose her on-screen costumes. Of course, they were always at the height of fashion, like the white tulle, flared skirt with embroidered waist and the black v-neck jumper worn in *The Rear Window*, a combination that was almost a manifesto for 1950s fashion. However, the real strength of her style is the fact that it transcends periods and fashions. In her recent *The Little Black Book of Style*, Nina Garcia, influential fashion director at *Marie Claire*, writes that every woman should see *To Catch a Thief* at least once in her life for tips on how to dress.

124 The actress poses for *Life* in an evening gown with a large floral print on the organza skirt.

126 A portrait of Grace Kelly from 1954, the year she filmed *The Country Girl*, which won her an Oscar.

The string of pearls, the cashmere turtle-neck sweater, the tailored tweed, and the silk chemise that the actress loved so much, are all now cornerstones of the female wardrobe. In fact, her favorite accessory has itself become synonymous with elegance: the Hermes bag now known as 'Kelly' in her honor. A handbag with a strap fastener, it was inspired by late 19th century saddlebags and invented by Robert Dumas in the 1930s. However, it only became a cult object when photographers captured it on the arm of the American star, who had just won an Oscar for George Seaton's *The Country Girl*.

So by the time she met Prince Ranieri of Monaco on 6 May 1955 during a photo shoot for Paris Match, Grace Kelly was already an icon. Her final 'consecration' though took place with their marriage on 19 April 1956 in the Cathedral of Saint Nicholas in Monte Carlo. The ceremony, which *TIME* magazine called the most romantic event since Romeo and Juliette, was broadcast on Eurovision. The bride wore a dress that made fashion history. It had a high-necked bodice, above a wide dress with a train. It was made from yards of taffeta, silk and old Brussels lace adorned with pearls. From her pearl-adorned hair hung a very long tulle veil designed by Helen Rose. The MGM costume designer dressed Kelly in her previous two films, *The Swan* and the musical *High Society*. With her marriage and farewell to Hollywood, the new princess started to look more European in that she began to prefer labels like Chanel, Givenchy, Grès, and Valentino over American ones like Oleg Cassini, whom she had dated. At the top of her list was Dior, thanks to her special connection with Marc Bohan, the house's creative director from 1961 to 1989. It appeared that the tailor of Grace's children, Princesses Caroline and Stephanie, and Prince Albert, dreamed up the Baby Dior line, launched in 1967. The former actress commented: "If there is one concept I can't relate to, it's that of shopping for the pleasure of it. Rather, I believe it right to honor all the people who create such beautiful things and give pleasure to those who see me wear them." Grace Kelly was adept at reconciling her more intimate family side with her position in society, transforming Monte Carlo into one of the most glamorous places on earth, thanks to the fabulous balls organized together with interior designer André Levasseur. Every appearance was an event, with her dresses, 19th century outfits, fluttering chiffon tunics, turbans, fur stoles, Van Cleef & Arpels diamond sets, and Cartier diadems. And, of course, the theatrical hairstyles created for her by Alexandre de Paris; they were architectural wonders of plaits and chignon all enhancing her already regal appearance. Hers was a regality that transcended all titles, because as Frank Sinatra said in 1956, "Grace Kelly was born a princess."

129 The Princess with one of the hairstyles created for her by Alexandre de Paris, the same stylist who did Liz Taylor's hair for *Cleopatra* (1963).

130 A V-neck top, a belted tutu skirt made of tulle and chiffon, white gloves, and a strand of pearls: in Alfred Hitchcock's *Rear Window* (1954), Grace Kelly embodies the more elegant side of '50s fashion. Oscar winner Edith Head came up with this oft-imitated outfit, inspired by Dior's New Look.

132 and 133 Grace Kelly is always impeccably dressed, even when she goes casual with no makeup. Here she's wearing a men's shirt, cuffed jeans, loafers, and a silk scarf in place of a belt.

134 The actress reads the script before shooting a scene. She was very nearsighted and often wore glasses (which she collected) when she wasn't on camera.

135 Grace Kelly in the French Riviera on the set of *To Catch a Thief* (1955), wearing a white bustier dress with several layers of chiffon, designed by Edith Head.

136 In 1955, the actress was used as a model for a line of mannequins.

137 The leading lady in a scene from *High Society* (1956), her last film. She has the engagement ring Prince Rainier gave her in 1956 on her finger: a 12 carat emerald-cut diamond.

138 and 139 The future princess in her 1955 Oscar gown, photographed by *Life*.

8

140-141 Grace in a black chemise, smiling at the photographers waiting for her on a New York street.

142-143 Grace and Prince Rainier at their wedding on April 19, 1956. The wedding gown designed by Helen Rose was a gift from MGM.

145   Grace chose a white taffeta gown with flowers along the neckline for her engagement party at New York's Waldorf-Astoria Hotel on January 6, 1956.

«PRINCES GRACE HAS BEQUEATHED US AN IMAGE OF IMMUTABLE ELEGANCE.»

·FRÉDÉRIC MITTERRAND·

146 and 147 Grace and her Hermès bag were inseparable. It was named Kelly after her. She even used it to hide the first signs of pregnancy from photographers in 1956. The Princess's other accessories include leather gloves, Ray-Ban Wayfarers, and scarves, always by Hermès.

149 Her Highness in 1954, in a dress decorated with fabric flowers. Her passion for all things floral led her to create collages of pressed flowers in her later years.

«MY MOTHER...EXUDED
EFFORTLESS ELEGANCE,
WHETHER SHE WAS APPEARING
AT THE MOST SPECTACULAR
PUBLIC OCCASION, OR A SIMPLE
FAMILY GATHERING.»

•PRINCE ALBERT OF MONACO•

JACQUELINE
KENNEDY

Simply Jackie   Simply Jackie

«Jacqueline Kennedy has given the American people one thing they have always lacked: Majesty.»

•London Evening Standard•

"We miss her," is how the New York Daily News bade farewell to Jacqueline Kennedy Onassis, a woman who lived three lives, when she passed in 1994. She was first the wife of the most beloved President of the United States; second, as a jetsetter, married to a famous and controversial Greek shipbuilder; and third, a woman finally free from cumbersome surnames (and husbands), known simply as 'Jackie.' Even now, previously unknown details of her life are coming to light (like the love story with brother-in-law Bobby Kennedy). She also had a huge influence on lifestyle for the last 50 years. Among the millions of hits under her name on the Internet, we find fashion sites and blogs instructing people how to dress like her. If you put on a pair of large sunglasses with dark lenses, fisherman's pants or a three-string pearl necklace you can easily look quite like the one and only true 'American Queen.' In reality, as Edward 'Ted' Kennedy recalled, "No one else had her style. No one talked like her, wrote like her, or was so original in the things she did." Jackie always emanated the same peerless class whether receiving a head of state or taking her children for a stroll in New York. This quality shined through even at the most difficult of times, including when she stood clearly upset, but not crying behind the coffin of John F. Kennedy, or when she flew to Paris to be photographed alongside Aristotle Onassis after his indulgent fling with Maria Callas.

However, it's her taste in clothes that remains firmly imprinted in the collective. "She never wore anything inelegant," wrote Tish Balridge in *A Lady First*, noting her rare ability to display the same nonchalance whether wearing an haute couture dress or a simple folk dress. Her 'good' origins certainly helped her. Jacqueline Lee Bouvier was born on 28 July 1929 to a family in Southampton, in New York State. Her mother, Janet Lee, the daughter of a very wealthy banker, was kept to the edges of high society due to her Irish roots. However, her father, John Vernou Bouvier III, descended from an old and powerful French family. Jackie went to the best schools and, after a year at the Sorbonne, graduated from George Washington University. She was not outstandingly beautiful, but she had grace and personality to spare. "I am five foot five tall, I have brown hair, a square face, and eyes so disgracefully distant from each other that it takes me three weeks to find a pair of glasses that fit my nose," she wrote in 1951 in a self-portrait for the *Prix de Paris*, a competition organized by Vogue. The prize was a contract as a correspondent in the French capital. Miss Bouvier won, but her mother stopped her from going. A first-rate decision, given that just a few months later, while she was working as a photo reporter for the Washington Times-Herald, she started going out with John Fitzgerald Kennedy, who she married in Newport in 1953.

"If there is a name that I don't want to be called it is First Lady. It makes me think of a racing horse," she declared shortly after her husband's election in November 1960. However, no politician's wife has ever filled this role

152 Jacqueline Kennedy in a sleeveless shift dress with little jewelry. Thirty years old and already so elegant.

154 The First Lady in Paris, in 1961.
Jackie wears a light yellow suit with one
of her famous pillbox hats to match.

better than Jackie, who between 1961 and 1963 transformed the image of the White House. She was helped in part by the sumptuous banquets created by Chef René Verdon and the interior restyling performed by decorator Henry ("Sister") Parish. However, it was Oleg Cassini, the Italian-Russian tailor with a US passport, who designed most of her 'state clothes,' as she liked to call them. These clothes were often as prominent on the front pages of the newspapers as were her husband's political decisions. Recall for a moment the pink bouclé woolen outfit (this time by Chanel) she wore in Dallas that became a symbol of 20th century history. "That wardrobe was an epidemic," declared Betty Ford, the wife of President Gerald Ford, emphasizing how women everywhere, American or not, began to dress in 'Jackie style.' Her day 'uniform' consisted of A-line frocks and dusters of the same cut and cloth. The alternative was a suit with a flared skirt cut below the knee, and a short, sack jacket with three quarter length sleeves and round neck, often without revers. There were no frills; even the buttons are almost always hidden. The motto 'less is more' also applied to evening wear, when the president's wife preferred long, sleeveless taffeta dresses, maybe softened by a bow and very few jewels (even though she owned fabulous Van Cleef & Arpels sets). At this time, Jackie loved intense colors (yellow, peach, and turquoise) and pillbox hats, invented by Roy Halston. For years, they were considered just as glamorous as her hairstyle, with the blunt cut and the backcombing on the top of her head, designed in 1960 by New Yorker Kenneth Battelle.

Having left the White House, Jackie's look was no longer constrained by official obligations. Her dresses shortened, her suits were often replaced by a black cashmere turtleneck, boat neck jerseys or patterned shirts, worn over white pants or Gap jeans. Even non-American designers were finally allowed in. Givenchy evening dresses returned to her wardrobe, along with Chanel jackets and Burberry trench coats. Then, there were the designs of a young Italian couturier, Valentino, who in 1968 designed the dress for her wedding on Skorpios with Aristotle Onassis. The gown featured beige lace corsage and tennis pleats. Sixty orders for exact same outfit were placed within a few days—and that's not counting the dozens of knock-offs flooding the market. Clearly, the former Mrs. Kennedy was as fashionable as she ever had been—if not more. This point is further demonstrated by the fact that one of the most desirable bags in the world is still the Gucci shoulder-bag with metal clasp that was renamed 'Jackie O' in her honor. She loved to wear it on its own or paired with a more precious mini bag. Other unmistakeable elements of her style include an Hermès scarf knotted under the chin, a Cartier watch, and the previously mentioned giant oval sunglasses. The same goes for the mass-produced leather sandals by Canfora, a simple shoemaker in Capri now legendary thanks to her.

157 For a visit to Lake Pichola in Udaipur, in Rajasthan, India, Jackie chose a pink taffeta dress with a bow at the waist, designed by Oleg Cassini.

158-159 Jackie in 1953, sporting a light shirt and Bermuda shorts while sailing with Senator John F. Kennedy, who was still her fiancé at the time. The couple shared a passion for the sea, and in the following years they would often be photographed aboard the family yacht, the *Honey Fitz*.

160 and 161 The Kennedys on their wedding day in Newport, September 12, 1953. The wedding gown is by New York designer Anne Lowe. The lace veil belonged to Jackie's grandmother.

162 A short-sleeved pullover and below-the-knee tartan skirt: Jackie salutes JFK before an American History class at Georgetown University, on September 3, 1954.

«HER STYLE WAS NOT VANITY
BUT A WAY OF LIVING,
NOT SIMPLY ADORNING HERSELF
BUT EXPRESSING HER VISION
OF BEAUTY IN THE WORLD».

•RICHARD MARTIN, COSTUME INSTITUTE, METROPOLITAN MUSEUM OF ART•

164-165   Jackie and Jack in New York on October 19, 1960, during his presidential campaign. The future First Lady is wearing a large overcoat with three-quarter length sleeves and a matching hat by Parisian designer Hubert de Givenchy. Long white gloves complete the look.

166 Jackie and Soviet Premier Niki-
ta Khrushchev during a dinner at the
Schönbrunn Palace in Vienna on
June 3, 1961. The beaded dress in
pink georgette is by Oleg Cassini.

167 Created by "state stylist" Oleg
Cassini, the pale blue crêpe bustier
dress with a bow at the neckline was
inspired by a Givenchy model who
appeared in *Femme Chic* in 1962.

168 Little John F. Kennedy Jr. (known as John-John) plays with his mother's pearls. Jackie alternated the three-strand necklace with a two-strand and a simple choker of larger pearls.

169 Jacqueline painting with her daughter, Caroline. Allowing glimpses into their private sphere, the Kennedys revolutionized the codes of political communication.

170 The essence of Jackie's style in the White House years (1961-1963): a small jacket over a flared dress, gloves, and a hat perched upon the widely copied hairstyle conceived by Kenneth Battelle.

171 After the White House: the former First Lady visits the Acropolis in Athens, in August 1969. She's wearing a shift dress that falls above the knee, jeweled sandals, and large sunglasses. Even her hair is less formal.

172 and 173 Impeccable even when she's relaxing on the beach. Side: Jackie on a boat with white pants and a scarf in her hair while vacationing in Amalfi, Italy in 1962. Left: on the Greek island of Skorpios, she walks barefoot along the port with her children, John and Caroline. And in 1968: the year she married shipping magnate Aristotle Onassis.

174 The "new" Jackie walks down Madison Avenue in New York, in October 1971, dressed casually: a flecked stretch wool pullover and faded pants that show off her fantastic figure.

175 New York, 1970. Mrs. Onassis leaving Bonwit Teller, a large department store that specializes in luxury shopping. The legendary "Jackie O" is visible on the shoulder of her trench coat: the Gucci shoulder bag launched in the '50s and made famous by Jackie in the following decade.

176-177 Jackie Kennedy in August 1959, at the age of 30. America's most beloved First Lady passed away in New York on May 19, 1994.

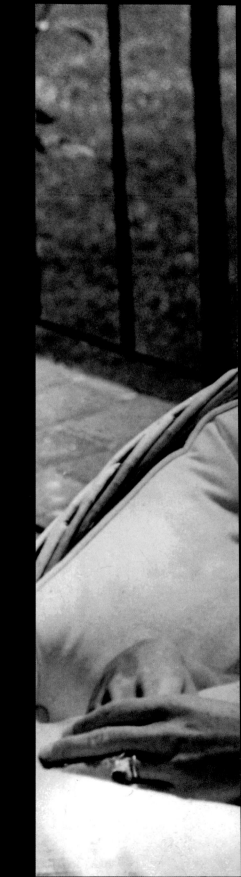

«JACKIE HAS BEEN A CONTINUING
SOURCE OF INSPIRATION.
SHE HAD EVERYTHING: CLASS,
STYLE, GRACE, CHARISMA,
AND SO MUCH COURAGE.»

•VALENTINO GARAVANI•

BRIGITTE
BARDOT

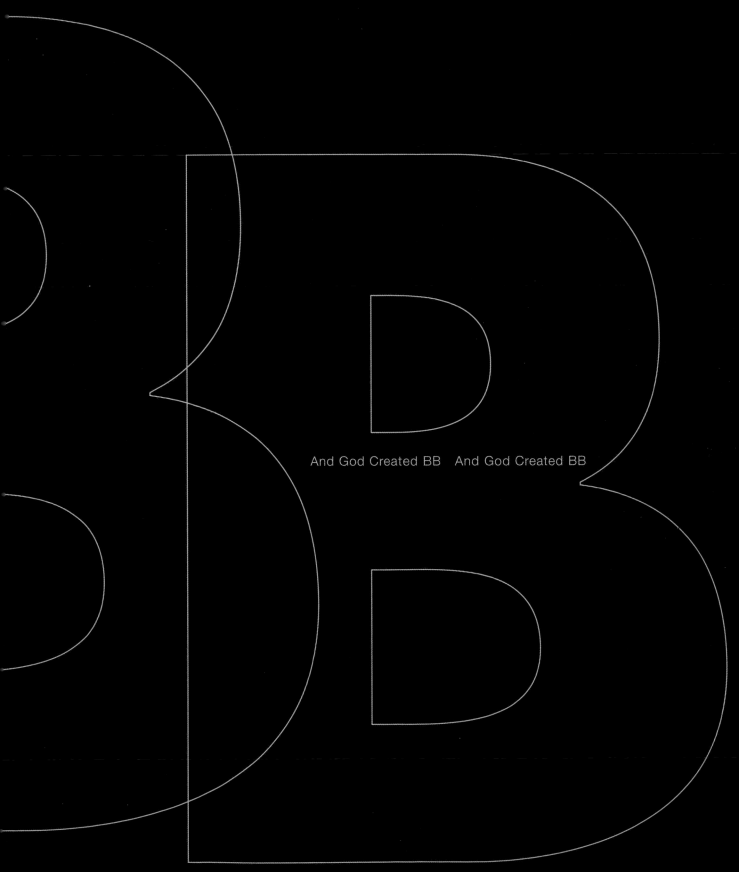
And God Created BB   And God Created BB

«I HAVE BEEN VERY HAPPY,
VERY RICH, VERY BEAUTIFUL,
MUCH ADULATED,
VERY FAMOUS AND
VERY UNHAPPY.»

•Brigitte Bardot•

In 1990, a young Claudia Schiffer made her debut at the Paris fashion shows; "and God recreated BB," said the newspapers, struck by her extraordinary resemblance to the star of the 50s and 60s. Journalist Giusi Ferré wrote "what nostalgia, what joy to see 'The Myth' again; to see that innocent look, that guilty mouth, the wild hair of Brigitte Bardot." Still, he came to the only possible conclusion: that there is only one BB.

However, the actress eventually turned her back on the past that made her so beloved and at the same time so unsatisfied. Perhaps it was this unhappiness that drove Brigitte to leave the cinema in 1973, after working with renowned directors like Louis Malle and Jean-Luc Godard, to dedicate herself exclusively to the defense of animal rights. She was 39 years old at the time and *Bardotlatrie* was still very much alive. Women imitated her and men dreamed about her. Just like in 1956, when the "little blond witch," as Jean Cocteau called her, enchanted everyone in the Roger Vadim film *And God Created Woman*.

Henry-Jean Servat, a writer and friend of the actress, commented: "It was post-war France, quiet, sleepy and conformist. She shook it all up." Brigitte was young, looked like a goddess, and was willing to undress on camera. And if that weren't enough, she was a sunny blonde, not the glacial type like Grace Kelly, who that year became Princess of Monaco. Bardot held an innocent and yet at the same time perverse fascination, a little like her character, Juliette, an uninhibited orphan who causes a commotion in the small fishing village of Saint Tropez. It became a favorite destination of the jet set, while Bardot became an international sex symbol and Europe's answer to Marilyn Monroe. The BB phenomenon took off; fans went mad at her every appearance, writers like Simone de Beauvoir explored the phenomenon, and Bob Dylan dedicated his first song to her. The Beatles were also mad about her, so much so that Cynthia Lennon dyed her hair to look like the French actress.

But who was this nymphet that many people had only just discovered, thinking that *And God Created Woman* was her first film? In reality, the girl had already shot 17 films and worked as a model since she was 15 years old. A Parisian, from a wealthy family (her father was the industrialist Louis Bardot), if she hadn't ended up on the cover of Elle, she would have continued studying dance and music at the conservatory. Instead, at 18 she made her debut on the big screen with *Le Trou Normand*. That same year, she married Roger Vadim, of whom she said "He was both my teacher and my partner. I placed myself totally in his hands." But if it's true that Vadim created BB, it's equally true to say that the actress did all the rest.

At 22 (years before the hippy era) she already shocked people with her eccentric habits. She wore jeans and a t-shirt, appearing barefoot in the most expensive restaurant in Paris (Chez Maxim's), and was photographed

180 Blond hair, heavy mascara, pink lip liner: BB in 1965.

182 BB in jeans, besieged by photographers in Cortina d'Ampezzo.

in Cannes wearing just a bikini. This garment became popular thanks to her, even though it was invented by French tailor Louis Reard in 1946. Indeed, the bikini languished unloved for a decade, thought to be too daring if not downright indecent. It took Bardot breaking the taboo about showing your belly button for the bikini to take off in America as well. However, BB took it further and went topless, showing off her perfect breasts on the beach at Saint Tropez, the symbolic home of the new hedonism with its parties and free love.

In the wake of this *Naughty Girl* (to mention a film of hers from 1958) she had the permanently *décontracté* air of someone who has just woken up after a late night out. First, there's her famous hair: very long, golden, fluffy, and artfully tousled. It seems that to achieve this effect, she washed it with dry shampoo rather than water. The desire to copy the look boosted hairspray sales, especially of *Elnett* by L'Oréal Paris, for which BB was a spokesperson. Indeed, without the right sort of lacquer it would have been impossible to attain her famous *choucroute*, that ruffled and back-combed look that symbolized the era. It was the same with her makeup: feline eyes, with black eyeliner and heavy mascara; thick, fleshy lips emphasized by a slightly darker pencil. As for clothes, fisherman's pants that finished just below the knee were a must for Bardot; low-cut jumpers that left her shoulders bare; and striped sailor's t-shirts, invented by Coco Chanel at the start of the century and relaunched by Brigitte in a sexy, new version. She draped herself in Vichy cloth in an incredibly sensual and much imitated fashion. Originally used for household linen, she transformed it into a sleeveless dress, belted tight around the waist. She wore blouses tied under her breasts and Sangallo lace bodices. Small checks (white and blue or white and pink) became Bardot's banner to the point that in June 1959, when she married her second husband, the actor Jacques Charrier, she wore a checkered Esterel dress.

With her slender body, BB was also perfect for 60s fashion, which finally showed the world her lovely legs. She began wearing miniskirts, shorts, and short dresses that she combined with *cuissardes* (over-the-knee boots), which she turned into a fashion phenomenon. However, the ballet flat is the shoe we most associate with Bardot. She championed this simple piece of footwear along with Audrey Hepburn, but to a completely different effect. On the feet of *Sabrina*, these flat shoes were tasteful; on Brigitte they appeared almost transgressive. It's no accident that she wore a pair painted bright red when dancing the mambo in a Vadim film. They were the Cinderella model, designed for the occasion by Rose Repetto, the mother of choreographer Roland Petit and owner of the historic brand that provides shoes for the Paris Opera. They are still fashionable half a century later.

185   October 1962, Saint Tropez. The actress sits on her new Caravelle S and plays with a dachshund puppy.

186 Brigitte Bardot talks with Pablo Picasso at the artist's studio in Vallauris, near Cannes, where the actress was invited to participate in the International Film Festival. It's 1956, the year she starred in *And God Created Woman*, directed by her husband Roger Vadim.

188   The pin-up version of the actress in 1958, in Saint Tropez, wearing a spaghetti strap bustier and very
tight shorts. Years of dancing shaped
her perfect body.

189   In 1961 Brigitte Bardot was in
Italy to finish filming A Very Private
Affair.

190 During a break on the set of *The Bride is Too Beautiful* the actress sports a version of the striped sailor's T-shirt, invented by Coco Chanel at the beginning of the century.

191 Brigitte's distinctive teased hair, which became a trend in the '60s, is still frequently imitated. Her secret is the expert build-up of layers.

192 BB leaving her Saint Tropez villa in a boat, the *Madrague*. She's wearing a basic bikini, which became popular in Europe and America because of her.

193 On May 29, 1967, the actress created a scandal by showing up at Chez Maxim's barefoot, in a caftan, with her third husband Gunther Sachs.

194 and 195 In 1966, Brigitte poses on the steps of a house in London, wearing a sweater, dark jeans and ankle boots. Bardot was a legend in England as well, to the point that the young Beatles wanted to make a film with her. In reality, John Lennon would only see her in person once, two years later at the Mayfair Hotel. But he was so overwhelmed he couldn't even talk to her.

196 BB hides under a beret with a large brim at the Zoom Zoom nightclub in Saint Tropez (1968).

197 December 1968. Bardot arrives at the London premiere of *Shalako*. She's chosen all black leather a mini trench coat, hat, and the *cuissardes* (over-the-knee boots) that became a phenomenon of the era.

198 BB on the set of *Shalako*, the 1968 Edward Dmytryk film.

199 A hippy-style Brigitte in August 1974, wearing a long printed dress with an underskirt. The leading lady plays the guitar, and is pictured here with a group of musicians at Club 55 in Saint-Tropez. As a singer, she recorded three albums and several singles in the '60s.

200 Bardot returning from Canada in 1977, where she waged a tough battle against clubbing baby seals for furs. Her biggest success was garnering the support of French President Valéry Giscard d'Estaing.

«Brigitte remains inimitable: with her ballet shoes, jeans, low necklines, the blonde bangs...She tried everything to destroy her own legend, but she couldn't do it.»

•Alberto Sordi•

MARY
QUANT

Swinging London   Swinging London

«Fashion is a tool to compete in life outside the home. People like you better, without knowing why, because people always react well to a person they like the looks of.»

•Mary Quant•

"Change was in the air and a young, brave English stylist, burst onto the scene. She was Mary Quant, the girl who didn't want to grow up and who, above all, didn't want to wear adult clothes. She brought us the miniskirt, colored socks and high boots along with the idea that young people must *never* at any cost, appear old. When Mary Quant was asked to explain the meaning and purpose of fashion, she gave an unambiguous answer: 'Sex.'"

This passage pretty well sums up the 1960s and is how Mary Higgins Clark, in her book *While My Pretty One Sleeps*, explains why she included Mary Quant, the only creative mentioned besides the peerless Mademoiselle Chanel. Like Coco, Mary was a revolutionary, a supporter of female emancipation. She helped women catch up with men. She didn't do this by reducing the difference between our and their wardrobe (this had already been done by Ms. *N°5*), but because, by making clothes sexier, she had also made women more desirable. The miniskirt ranks high among items with an erotic association. Indeed it is impossible to talk about this iconic garment without mentioning Quant, who many see as the inventor. However another stylist, Andre Courrèges also claimed paternity, shocking haute couture with an above the knee dress at a famous 1964 fashion show. Of course, it doesn't really matter who first chopped a few inches off skirt lengths: the only thing for sure is that without Mary Quant and her Bazaar boutique on London's Kings Road, that foot of cloth would not have become the story of an entire generation.

"The real creators are the girls, the ones you see on the street," commented Quant diplomatically while she used a young student-model to promote her work. The girl was Lesley Hornby, otherwise known as Twiggy. Those were the Swinging Sixties in the *trendiest* (a term dating from this era) city in the world: London. The London of the Mods (or Modernists) with their parkas and customized scooters, described by the cult film *Quadrophenia*; the London of Beatlemania that, in 1964, also took off in the United States; the London of Carnaby Street with its independent music shops and street-fashion clothing shops. In a single word: *camp*. Camp London was exclusive, extravagant, and feverish. "Camp is to be at the height of fashion. Camp is to be a famous cover girl, the husband of a princess, a photographed photographer, a pop singer," wrote Lietta Tornabuoni in 'L'Europeo' in 1966, pointing to Mary Quant as the 'torchbearer' of this youthful revolt that revitalized England, conquered Europe and now influences the big French fashion houses.

No one could argue that the stylist was anything other than non-conformist. Born in 1934, the daugh-

204 The designer among fabrics. In 1955, she opened her first boutique, Bazaar, on Kings Road in London.

206 Mary Quant poses between two models in miniskirts, of which she was considered the inventor.

ter of two university teachers, she left home at 16 to live a Bohemian life in the capital. This is where she met her future husband, aristocrat, Alexander Plunkett-Greene, who was, like her, keen on freedom and change. In 1955, after studying at Goldsmiths College, Mary opened her first boutique, Bazaar, in Chelsea. Within a short time the store became a must for celebrities who were attracted by her shocking and affordable creations. "Snobbery is unfashionable and in our shops duchesses are to be found rubbing up alongside typists buying the same clothes," commented Mary who, in 1963 founded the Ginger Group to export her collections to America. Three years later, she received an Order of the British Empire from Queen Elizabeth. The miniskirt, her *pièce de résistance*, later received recognition on a Royal Mail stamp in 2008.

Generally, miniskirts were flared, smooth or with tennis pleats, black, optical motifs or in bright colors, like red, lemon yellow and fuchsia. It is worn with a roll-neck pullover, a simple T-shirt or a cardigan with a zipper. The alternative version is a similarly short dress, either trapeze-line or body hugging, like an oversized T-shirt. One example is the football dress, an elasticated jersey dress inspired by soccer kits launched by Quant in 1967, when the miniskirt was already a certain hit. This success was due in part to famous fans like the beautiful Florinda Bolkan, the shoeless singer Sandie Shaw, and supermodels Veruschka, Jean Shrimpton and Elsa Martinella. Even Jackie Kennedy, the most tasteful of 60s icons, gave in to the miniskirt. Then, of course, there was Audrey Hepburn, who again in 1967, with her film *Two for the Road*, amazed the world by betraying her made-to-measure Givenchy clothes for Mary Quant's off-the-peg products.

Other fashion 'revolutions' were also linked to Mary Quant. Higher hems forced a radical change in lingerie, making it impossible to use garters. So along with the mini, the English stylist brought out the newly invented thick tights, preferably in colors or with designs (she was the first to produce them with her own logo, a daisy, which appeared before the flower power movement). She also produced above-the-knee boots, the so-called *cuissard* made famous by Jane Fonda in Barbarella. However, her most famous shoe was the square toed pump with an ankle strap, either painted or in transparent rubber. Her passion for new, synthetic fibers was already obvious in 1963 when, on the occasion of her first Paris fashion show, she created the futuristic *Wet Collection*; a series of PVC dresses and small raincoats in bold colors. She wore these clothes herself, along with the memorable beret and bulls-eye gloves, true marks of her style. Then, there was the haircut created for her by another iconic of Swinging London, hairdresser Vidal Sassoon. His five-point cut, very short hair, perfectly geometric and with a fringe covering the eyebrows, was one of the most imitated of the era and certainly contributed to elevating Mary Quant to iconic status. Or better, as she was called by the writer Bernard Levin, "the high priestess of 60s fashion."

210-211 Quant in October 1967, discussing the prototype of a new plastic shoe with her husband, Alexander Plunkett-Greene. In 1963, the two of them founded the Ginger Group to export their creations to the U.S. The brand was acquired by a Japanese company in 2000.

211 On November 15, 1966, Mary happily shows the press her Officer of the British Empire badge, which she'd just received directly from the Queen at Buckingham Palace. For the occasion, the designer wore a white wool jersey mini dress with a zipper and contrasting stitching.

213 The designer, at the age of 30, lying on a wicker couch and sketching. The daughter of two professors, she studied at Goldsmiths College.

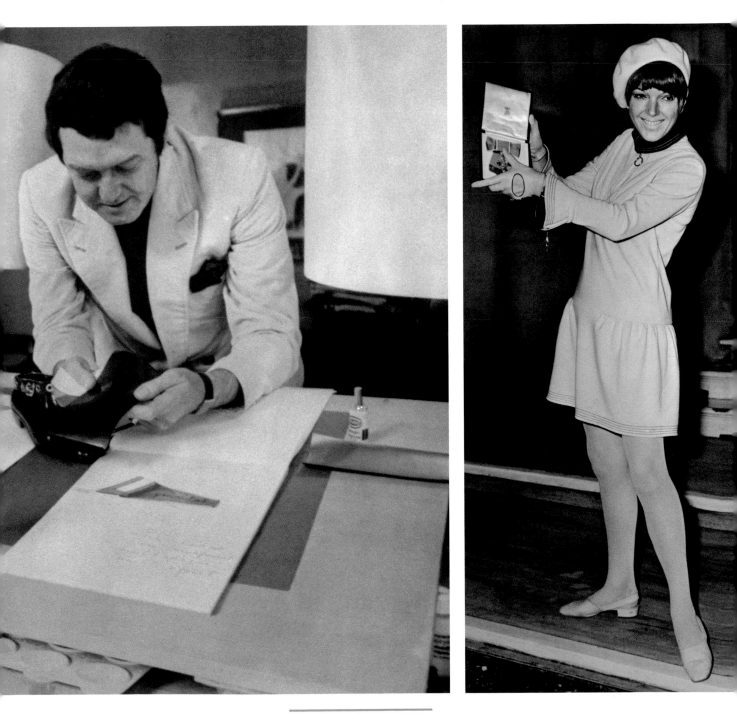

«A FASHIONABLE WOMAN
WEARS CLOTHES;
THE CLOTHES DON'T WEAR HER.»

•MARY QUANT•

214-215 Mary and a group of models (strictly in miniskirts) at London's Heathrow airport on March 18, 1968, waiting to leave for a European fashion tour.

MARY QUANT Swinging London

216-217 At her workshop in 1964, Mary Quant oversees the making of a pair of flounce shorts, the year before she won the Sunday Times International Award for the worldwide success of her young, innovative fashion.

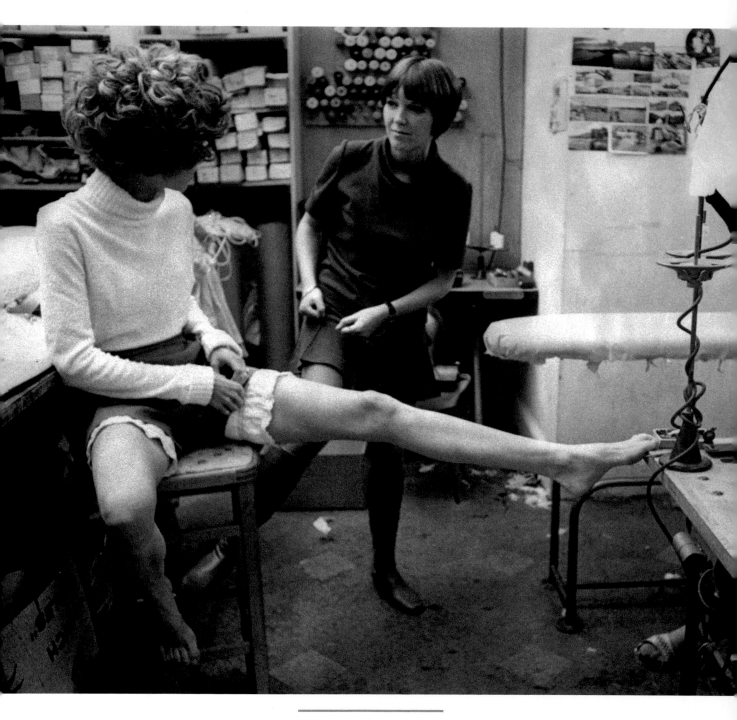

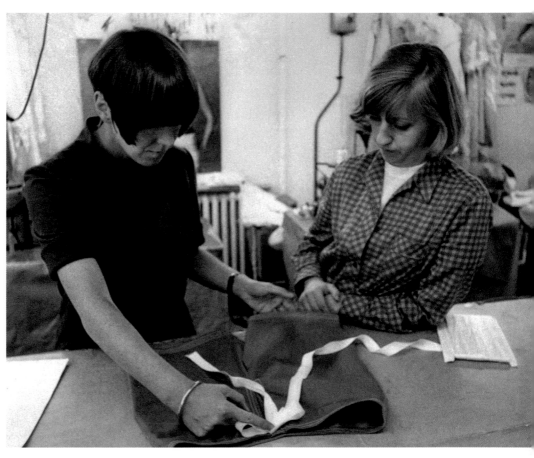

218-219 and 219 The designer, along with dressmakers and a model, at two different moments in the process of working on the new collection in 1967.

220 and 221 Fashion publications adore Mary. On the left, young models wear her famous mini dresses. Each one has a Basque-style beret (indulging Quant's hat fetish) and a pair of colored tights. On the right, the designer launches the plastic ankle boot.

223 Quant with her distinctive bob, which she still sports today.

IS THIS JUST ANOTHER FAD?

The big beret.

12s 6d.

12 Quant colours.

Enquiries
for Quant berets
to
39 Fitzroy
Square,
London W1.

MARY QUANT

quant
takes that brilliance
to boots!

With quant afoot—boots with a difference in a sparkling first collection of shiny-bright boots by Mary Quant. In crystal clear plastic over colours that zoom into fashion's orbit, they're boots that shrug off wear and weather marks, come up shining. Five different styles, all with the uncluttered, unmistakable Quant touch, all in a choice of colours, all from sizes 3, 3½, right up to 7. The shiny red plastic bag is free—and, for the girl who likes things neat and tidy, there's a quant afoot cotton shoe bag in five different colours for 5/- each. Just watch quant afoot boots start walking, all over town.

1 & 6 'Zip' 6 colours 49/11
2 'Porthole' 4 colours 49/11
3 'Cuff' 3 colours 49/11
4 'Chelseas' 4 colours 49/11
5 'Daddy Long Legs' 4 colours 79/11

quant afoot
by mary quant

Mary Quant Footwear Ltd
3 Ives Street, Chelsea
London SW3

«The Look isn't just the
garments you wear.
It's the way you put
your makeup on,
the way you do your hair,
the sort of stockings
you choose,
the way you walk
and stand.»

•Mary Quant•

TWIGGY

The Face of the Sixties

«At sixteen I was a funny,
skinny little thing,
all eyelashes and legs.
And then, suddenly people
told me it was gorgeous.
I thought they had
gone mad.»

·Twiggy·

London's National Portrait Gallery dedicated a show to Twiggy to celebrate her 60th birthday on 19 September 2009. It included photographs of her by giants of photography, including Richard Avedon, Cecil Beaton, Bert Stern, and Douglas Kirkland. This was a fitting tribute for the world's first real top model and one of the most famous Englishwomen of all time. Like the Beatles, the Rolling Stones and the Mini Cooper, Twiggy was a symbol of British style, or more precisely of the "Swinging Sixties;" an era of extraordinary change in fashion and culture that put London at the center of the world. With her blue eyes and a look of an eternally sulky girl, Twiggy unknowingly came to incarnate the whole scene: youth revolution, street fashions and pop music. However, the word incarnate, which means "embodied in flesh," is hardly appropriate for her. At the peak of her career, she weighed little more than 88 pounds (40 kg), which is why she was jokingly nicknamed 'Twiggy.'

The real name of the woman who changed the canon of female aesthetics was Lesley Hornby, born in 1949 in working class Neasden in London. Mary Quant first discovered her in 1964 when she decided that the young models slim body would be ideal for promoting the miniskirt, but the official beginning of the Twiggy legend dates to 1966. In her account, it all happened one January afternoon in Mayfair, at the salon of fashionable hairdresser Leonard Lewis. Photographer Barry Lategan needed to take some shots for new salon posters. A young, 18-year-old student, the daughter of a carpenter and a check-out girl at Woolworths, was one of the models. "It was all so exciting!" recalls Twiggy, who had to go through seven endless hours of cutting and coloring as the hairdresser tried to make up his mind. However, the wait was worth it. The end result was a short, very tidy cut, with a left part, and her locks lightened to a warm honey color. She did her own make-up, leaving her freckles very visible and enlarging the bottom eyelashes with skillful pen strokes and a massive application of mascara. Twiggy looked like a boy on his first day at school, an intriguing asexual creature. Lategan's portrait became the manifesto for an entire generation, the Mods (or Modernists), scathing of anything that wasn't new, young, different and fun. Within just a few weeks, the United Kingdom was full of Twiggy clones. This was also thanks in part to Daily Express journalist Deirdre McSharry, who saw the photograph at Leonard Lewis' and proclaimed Twiggy "The Face of 1966."

From that point she became famous worldwide; magazines like Vogue, Newsweek and Harpers Bazar wanted her on the cover. Her immature, boyish body was perfect for the fashion of Courrège, Cardin and Ungaro; the clean lines, geometrical designs, masculine style pieces and, naturally, the very short hems, which sat gid-

226 A mini yellow chemise, flowered tie and white loafers: the English model poses with a look from the Twiggy Dresses collection, launched in 1966.

228 During a press conference in New York in 1967, Leonard of London retouches the famous cut with which he "invented" Twiggy.

231 Twiggy stands with her legs apart, in a pleated, flared lamé dress and silver pumps during a shoot in New York in 1967.

dily at the top of her spindly legs. Today, when most runway models are a size two, her legs would create no particular impression. However, in the 60s they were a sensation. With the exception of Audrey Hepburn, before Twiggy, people were captivated by beautiful and voluptuous cinema stars like Marilyn Monroe and Sophia Loren, or svelte (but never underweight) and elegant icons such as Jackie Kennedy and Grace Kelly. Even models had curvaceous bodies.

Twiggy changed everything; these tiny sizes became a mark of beauty that girls pursued. Girls the world over wanted to look like Twiggy. In order to achieve the look, they submitted to exhausting and largely useless diets—without accounting for the fact that Hornby was naturally slim. Of course, this created uproar. Some of the press said she had "the body of a starving person with the face of an angel." There were innumerable jokes about her skin and bone appearance and even a doctor, Professor Bernbeck from Hamburg, railed against her, accusing her of being ill. However, Twiggy was popular because she was on the edge between woman and girl, masculine and feminine, slimness and anorexia. She was the icon of a new female emancipation. Mattel marketed a doll that looked like her; false eyelashes and socks with her name went on sale; and she had her own line of clothes, Twiggy Dresses, aimed at a very young market. The collection included a micro shirtwaist dress with a military cut to be worn with flowery necktie scarves, A-line dresses with hoods, sleeveless pullovers, spangled short skirts, moccasins, fringed boots, and painted shoes with square toes and low heels.

While teenagers appropriated her style, she began to look beyond fashion. At just 20 years old and only three years into her dazzling career, the model who inspired Michelangelo Antonioni's *Blow Up* (1966) and without ever appearing on a catwalk (at that time fashion shows were considered low-level work for models), left modeling and went into films. Her acting debut in Ken Russell's musical *The Boy Friend* (1971) was a success, winning her two Golden Globe awards in 1972 (New Star of the Year - Actress and Best Actress in a Musical or Comedy). In the following years, she appeared in the theater and on television, and also made music, her lifelong passion (her first single, 'Beautiful Dreams,' came out in 1966). In answer to the question of why she so quickly left the fashion system, she quipped: "You can't be a clothes hanger for your entire life." However, one thing is certain: without Twiggy, Kate Moss and other slimline models would never have reached the top.

232 For her distinctive eyes, Twiggy (who does her own makeup) covers her eyelids in white, and then adds eye shadow and eye liner. Finally, she adds three pairs of fake eyelashes.

233 A close up of the haircut that transformed Lesley Hornby into Twiggy.

234 and 235 Twiggy at a photo shoot in London, in 1966.

236 and 237 The English cover girl embodies the new '60s fashion. On the left, a crochet dress with drawstring waist. On the right, a laminated jersey shift dress with a high neck.

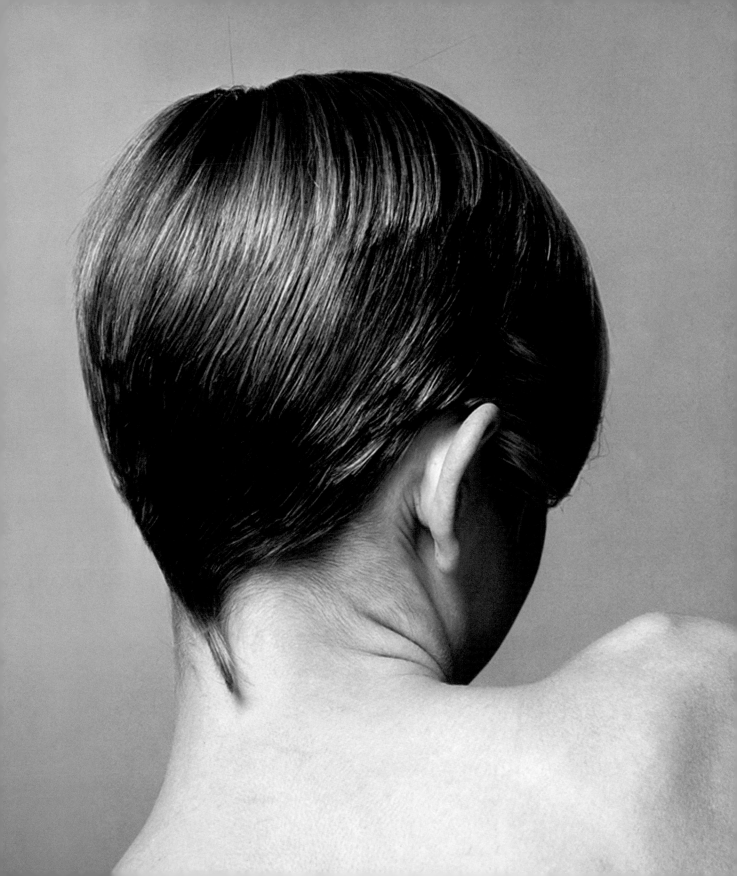

238 and 239 Two Swinging London style accessories: large two-tone sunglasses and gloves with a hole cut out.

240 and 241 Above: Twiggy in a pink sack dress with buttons at the neck and large silver ball earrings. Right: Twiggy with a fake braid in an unpublished photo from a 1966 news article.

243 The model on the cover of *British Vogue* in 1967. After working just one year, she's already an icon to teenagers all over the world and Mattel is about to make a Twiggy Barbie.

«Why did I retire?
You can't be a clothes
hanger for
your entire life.»

·TWIGGY·

VOGUE

OCTOBER 15 1967 4/-

GREAT NEW LOOKS

WITH MORE THAN
A DASH OF FLATTERY

BEAUTY
THROUGH A
MAGNIFYING GLASS

WHAT'S NEW IN PRINT:
CASHMERE

ELIZABETH AND
RICHARD BURTON
OBSERVATIONS
BY A FAMOUS DIRECTOR

AUSTRALIA:
THE LUCKY COUNTRY

DIANA
SPENCER

The Glamour Princess
The Glamour Princess

«Don't call me an icon, I'm only a mother.»

•Lady Diana•

In the 80s and 90s, Princess Diana, universally known first as Lady and then Princess Di, was the most photographed woman in the world. Any dress she wore was reviewed, criticized, admired and copied. Despite personal reserves, she became an undisputed model of elegance and style. She was consecrated as such by one of the most renowned and authoritative fashion writers, Colin McDowell, who in 2007, ten years after her death, published his book *Diana Style*. The Sunday Times writer declared that "her every choice in fashion had an enormous influence," adding however, that England's lost queen only found her own style in the last phase of her life. We have a fantastic record of this thanks to the work of great photographers like Mario Testino. However, when she first appeared in the public eye, the woman who changed the image of the British crown gave no hint of her future as a glamorous princess. On the contrary, the press criticized her wardrobe of flouncy blouses, flowery dresses, polka dots, pumps and regulation pearls.

In 1981, when she became engaged to Prince Charles, Diana Frances Spencer had the typical, slightly old-fashioned wardrobe of an upper class girl. She was also so intensely shy and reserved that she looked almost ungainly—despite her height and attractive features. That aside, she was just 19 years old, the daughter of one of the oldest and noblest families of the British aristocracy, who had received a very traditional education. In brief, she was exactly what the royal family was after: a young, aristocratic, virgin bride. But she was also something the world wanted: a new fairy tale about a 'simple' girl who becomes a princess by marrying the man she loves. The Royal Wedding, on 29 July of the same year, at St. Paul's Cathedral in London, was dubbed the marriage of the century, a title previously enjoyed by the nuptials of Grace Kelly and Prince Ranieri of Monaco. It was a worldwide media event watched by 800 million television viewers. Diana's dress was entirely British made and combined romanticism with an almost hint of Disney. It was made from silk taffeta and old lace, with big puff sleeves and ten petticoats. The veil was 23 feet (7 meters) long and embellished with 10 thousand pearls. Naturally, not everyone liked it and some people called it the 'meringue dress.' However, the fact is that Elizabeth Emanuel's creation entered history along with the Princess of Wales and revived the fashion for elaborate wedding dresses after years of simpler and often shorter ones.

Following the wedding, Diana's style became more sophisticated, thanks in part to the advice of the staff of Vogue UK. She gradually abandoned the puffed sleeves and balloon dresses. Her silhouette shrank and floral patterns alternated with plaids and solid colors. During the day she wore suits with a tubular skirt and in the evening, dresses with slenderizing lines. She lightened her hair, which she kept short and layered, and wore proper ladies' hats, which had-

246 Diana Spencer in the mid-1990s, after her divorce from Charles.

248 Princess Diana with the famous Elvis Look designed by Catherine Walker.

n't been seen for many years. One constant though, mostly for reasons of protocol, was her preference for British brands that, thanks to her, became renowned worldwide. Designer Bruce Oldfield called her a real 'English Rose': "a very simple woman, who put on no airs and who was open to suggestions." Diana also favored Arabella Pollen, Amanda Wakeley and Catherine Walker. Christie's auctioned many pieces by these designers for charity following Princess Di's death in the Alma Tunnel in Paris.

But let's take a step back to the early 90s and the end of the royal fairy tale. On 5 December 1992, Charles and Diana separated, after the birth of two sons (William and Harry) and serial unfaithfulness. The transformation of the Princess from 'English Rose' to global style icon had already begun, but the turning point was a red Valentino cocktail dress that Her Highness 'dared' to wear on a state visit to France, thus betraying her usual British designers. Close fitting, with a velvet bodice and lace dress down to the knee, it was far from the virginal (and pastel toned) look of her early period. Like other creations by the Italian tailor, which she wore in private, Princess Di ordered this model over the phone and he made it using a mannequin with her measurements, jealously guarded in his Roman workshop. Speaking to *La Repubblica* newspaper the couturier declared "I think it an act of bravery by an extraordinary woman who in her own way is trying to modernize old obsolete rules." He added that no one in the world could wear his dresses better than the princess. He was not the only one to think so. At the time, an opinion poll showed her to be the most popular member of the royal family; all of the top designers were competing to dress her. This was also because she was more beautiful than when she was 20 years old. More image conscious, she now had the body of a model, sculpted by her daily early morning swims—but also unfortunately by bulimia, to which she confessed.

From John Galliano to Giorgio Armani, Christian Lacroix to Karl Lagerfeld for Chanel, so many people contributed to the creation of the image of the new Princess Di, who dominated the jet set from on high with her Jimmy Choo shoes. However, no one knew how to bring out her sexy side better than Gianni Versace, who designed several of her most memorable outfits. One of these was a grey pearl silk siren dress, completely covered in little pearls and metallic details, immortalized by the Patrick Demarchelier painting. There was also a pink pantsuit worn in 1995 for an official military occasion. The small, double-breasted short sleeve jacked and the pillbox hat were a clear sign that the couturier saw Diana as the new Jackie Kennedy. Unfortunately, a tragic fate awaited them both. They died within a few weeks of each other in the summer of 1997. At Gianni's funeral, Diana, the 'Queen of Hearts,' carried the handbag with a golden medusa, dedicated to her by the stylist. It wasn't the only one: two years earlier there had already been the Lady Dior and the D Bag by Tod's.

251 Diana attends a military parade in 1991, wearing a satin dress that reflects the image of the English Rose.

252 Sketches of Diana's wedding gown, created by Elizabeth Emanuel and her husband David.

253 The Princess after saying "Yes." It took three months to make the dress, in an atelier swarmed by paparazzi.

Wedding Gown of The Lady Diana Spencer

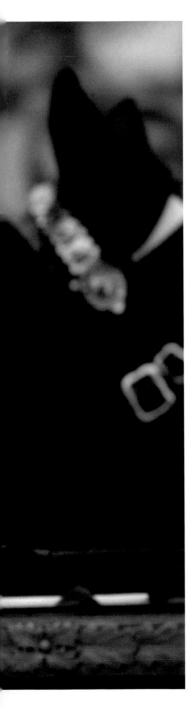

254-255 Diana and Charles at St. Paul's Cathedral in London on their wedding day: July 29, 1981. The bride, who'd turned 20 on July 1st, arrived at the ceremony in a carriage. It turned out to be too small for her large gown of taffeta and antique lace with its 23-foot (7-meter) veil.

LADY DIANA The glamour princess

256-257   Lady Di sports a wide-brimmed straw hat by Frederick Fox on a trip to Anzio, Italy in 1985. Though it was often required by etiquette, the Princess loved this particular accessory. In fact, it came back in style thanks to her, and not just for official occasions.

258-259 To visit the English Army in 1995, Diana chose a pink suit by Gianni Versace, the designer who understood better than anyone how to capture her charm in the last few years of her life. The cut of the jacket, along with the hat, is clearly homage to Jackie Kennedy's style.

260 Another suit with a one-button blazer for Diana Spencer, photographed in 1990. White was one of her favorite colors, along with red.

«BEAUTIFUL, ELEGANT, CHARMING,
VERY STYLISH, AND A
WONDERFUL MOTHER.»

·JACQUELINE KENNEDY ONASSIS·

262-263 Lady Di in her daytime 'uni-form': the suit. The cut of her jackets became tighter and more masculine over the years, compared to previous versions with puffy sleeves. She usually didn't wear a blouse, she wore a vest instead.

265 The Princess in a light blue chiffon dress with draped bodice and matching scarf: a Catherine Walker creation from 1987.

«She was very charismatic
as a person, not just because
she was a princess. She had
this caring quality.
She had compassion.»

·David Sassoon·

266 Lady Di arrives at Royal Albert Hall in London, wearing a blue and white cocktail dress with jeweled buttons. According to the *Metropolitan Post*, she had over three thousand designer outfits.

267 At a gala dinner for cancer research on November 20, 1995, Diana wears a low-cut Jacques Azagury dress and an extravagant pearl choker with a large sapphire surrounded by diamonds.

269 Diana in 1995, two years before her premature passing on August 31, 1997. Many of her clothes have been auctioned off for charity since then.

«I ALWAYS FELT SHE REALLY
UNDERSTOOD HOW TO USE
FASHION AS A SILENT LANGUAGE
AND LET CLOTHES DO THE
TALKING FOR HER WHEN SHE
COULDN'T, THE WAY A MOVIE
STAR IN THE SILENT FILMS DID».

•JOHN GALLIANO•

authors

Valeria Manferto De Fabianis graduated in Philosophy at the Università Cattolica del Sacro Cuore in Milan. She is an expert in photographic editing and image creation. In 1984, together with Marcello Bertinetti, she founded Edizioni White Star where she took on the position of Editorial Director. Her books include: *Fidel Castro, El Líder Máximo – A Life in Picture*, *John Lennon – In his Life* and *Fur and feathers... an unusual farm*.

Paola Saltari graduated in Political Science at the University of Bologna with a thesis on Sociology in Fashion, and she gained a Masters degree in Communication at the European Fashion School in Milan, before becoming a professional journalist. From 2003 she has been part on the editorial staff of "Vanity Fair" where she is deputy head of Style.

Anna Molinari's world is one of seduction and charm, great vitality and a spontaneous sense of fun. The designer in three decades of creativity has conquered the fashion world. She has created clothes considered true cult items, such as the t-shirts with logo in Swarovski crystals or the famous Blu-Vi, the small cardigan in cashmere with a mink collar, photographed on the greatest Hollywood stars. Anna Molinari has assigned Blumarine AD campaigns to camera wizards such as Helmut Newton and Albert Watson, photographing top models of the calibre of Naomi Campbell, Cindy Crawford, Eva Herzigova, Helena Christensen, Carla Bruni, Carré Otis and Monica Bellucci.

The Editor wishes to thank:
JFK Presidential Library and Museum, Boston; Press Office Parfums Beauté Chanel, Milan; Press Office Prince's Palace of Monaco; Katharine Houghton Hepburn Center, Bryn Mawr (Pennsylvania) for their invaluable help

WS White Star Publishers® is a registered trademark property of White Star s.r.l.

© 2010, 2018 White Star s.r.l.
Piazzale Luigi Cadorna, 6
20123 Milan, Italy
www.whitestar.it

Revised edition

Translation: Alan Goldwater (texts) - Mary Doyle (captions)
Editing: Sarah M K Mastrian

«ELEGANCE IS THE ONLY BEAUTY THAT NEVER FADES.»

•AUDREY HEPBURN•